GREAT HOUSES
OF ENGLAND
& WALES

Concise Edition

GREAT HOUSES OF ENGLAND & WALES

HUGH MONTGOMERY-MASSINGBERD
CHRISTOPHER SIMON SYKES

Laurence King

ACKNOWLEDGEMENTS

We received wonderfully generous help, hospitality and advice from many owners, friends, administrators and experts, and we would particularly like to thank the following, all of whom have made significant contributions to the book and to our enjoyment in producing it: Julian Bannerman, the Marquess of Bath, Mark Bence-Jones, Laura Beresford, the Duke of Buccleuch, the Earl of Burlington, the late William and Sarah Bulwer-Long, John Chesshyre, the Marquess of Cholmondeley, Susan Cleaver, Alec Cobbe, Selina Coghlan, Sophie Collins, Jacky Colliss Harvey, Philip Cooper, Jon Culverhouse, Lady Victoria Cuthbert, Warren Davis, Viscount and Viscountess De L'Isle, the Duke and Duchess of Devonshire, Paul Duffie, Howard Eaton, Lord and Lady Egremont, Terry Empson, Gareth Fitzpatrick, David Freeman, Christopher Gilbert, Philippa Glanville, the Knight of Glin, Rosamund Griffin, the Earl and Countess of Harewood, John Harris, Min Hogg, Sandra Howat, Simon Howard, Karen Howes, Norman Hudson, St Clair Hughes, Robert Innes-Smith, Gervase Jackson-Stops, John Kenworthy-Browne, the late John Langton, the Marquess of Lansdowne, the late W.R. de W. Lash, Lady Victoria Leatham, the late James Lees-Milne, the Earl and Countess of Leicester, Cynthia Lewis, Candida Lycett Green, Helen Marchant, the Duke and Duchess of Marlborough, Luke Massingberd, John Montgomery-Massingberd, Teresa Moore, the Duke of Northumberland, Dr Diane Owen, the Earl of Pembroke, George Plumptre, Peter Reid, Dr C.L. Ridgway, John Martin Robinson, Lord Rothschild, Christopher Rowell, Cosmo Russell, Graham Rust, the Duke of Rutland, Lord Sackville, Hugh and Bridget Sackville-West, Peter Sinclair, Karen Stafford, Freddie Stockdale, Sir Tatton Sykes Bt, the Marquess and Marchioness of Tavistock, the Reverend Miles Thomson, the Reverend Henry Thorold, Hugo Vickers, David Watkin, Lavinia Wellacombe and Lady Willoughby de Eresby.

Published in 2000 by Laurence King Publishing
an imprint of Calmann & King Ltd
71 Great Russell Street
London WC1B 3BN
Telephone: +44 20 7831 6351
Fax: +44 20 7831 8356
e-mail: enquiries@calmann-king.co.uk
www.laurence-king.com

A catalogue record for this book is available from the British Library.

ISBN 1 85669 206 X

Designed by Karen Stafford

Printed in China

Half title: Ocular panels by Colin Gill at Blenheim Palace, Oxfordshire.
Frontispiece: Longleat, Wiltshire.

CONTENTS

INTRODUCTION

Let us see these handsome houses
Where the wealthy nobles dwell

TENNYSON, *The Lord of Burleigh*

IN HIS stories about the adventures of the eccentric Earl of Emsworth, P.G. Wodehouse painted a beguiling picture of surely the *beau idéal* of a great house of England and Wales (indeed, conveniently situated around the border between the two countries), Blandings Castle, which dates from a time, as the author tells us, when the landed gentry 'believed in building their little nests solid'. The understatement is, of course, deliberate, for the 'huge, grey and majestic' Blandings, family seat of the Threepwoods, 'unquestionably takes the eye'.

We are told of its turrets, battlements and stone terrace with its curved balustrade; the celebrated library (with, among other treasures, the Mazarin Bible attributed to Johann Gutenberg); the Picture Gallery, hung with Threepwood family portraits (one notably improved by the present Earl's revolver); and the Amber Drawing Room, with its remarkably early landscape of the Vale of Blandings by Pourbus (Franz the Younger?). We are led up to the tapestried bedrooms (slept in by Tudor monarchs on their progresses) and down

to the butler's pantry. Outside, on a sultry summer afternoon, we can marvel at the famous rose garden, the lake, the deer park and, in the corner of a buttercup meadow, the sty of Lord Emsworth's own beloved sow, the Empress of Blandings, the Noblest of her Species.

It all sounds like paradise. As Evelyn Waugh observed, 'The gardens of Blandings Castle are that original garden from which we are all exiled'. Waugh himself created an irresistible vision of a later, Baroque, great house in his novel *Brideshead Revisited*, the seat of the Flytes, Marquesses of Marchmain, with its classical lodges, picturesque landscape, dome and columns, fountain, temple and obelisk.

Were these figments of the Wodehousian and Wavian imaginations merely idyllic fantasies, or were they approximations of the truth? Waugh wrote *Brideshead* during the Second World War, when it seemed, as he put it in the preface to the revised edition of 1959, 'that the ancestral seats which were our chief national artistic achievement were doomed to decay and spoliation like the monasteries in the 16th century'. So, as he said, he 'piled it on rather, with passionate sincerity'.

Yet, after revisiting the 25 great houses of England and Wales featured in this book, and

PRECEDING PAGES
'Brideshead', alias Castle Howard, across the lake.

BELOW
A pepper pot roofscape at Burghley House.

By the end of the 1950s Waugh considered that 'Brideshead today would be open to trippers, its treasures rearranged by expert hands and the fabric better maintained than it was by Lord Marchmain'. Certainly the 'cult of the country house' and the ubiquitous 'expert hands' have done a great deal of good in focusing attention on the artistic importance of these buildings and their collections. Previous pictorial surveys, however, have tended to view great houses purely in terms of arts and crafts, as if they were merely museums dumped in the middle of a field and belonging to an ancient and long-vanished civilization.

We have preferred to look at them as they are today, at the dawn of the 21st century, in their present ownership. While the text gives due credit to the architects, artists and craftsmen employed on their creation, greater emphasis is laid on the

BELOW
Bess of Hardwick in pride of place above her son, the 1st Earl of Devonshire at Hardwick Hall.

looking at the illustrations laid out on the pages that follow, one can only conclude that the Eden represented by Blandings and Brideshead is far from an illusion. Indeed, there are evocative whiffs of Blandings at Powis Castle and Penshurst Place, and of Brideshead at Castle Howard.

As Waugh observed, it was impossible to foresee in the 1940s – that drearily utilitarian and egalitarian decade – the 'present cult of the country house'. The Second World War and its austere aftermath led to the destruction of many houses. Yet, as Sir Osbert Sitwell noted, 'Alas! how curious it is that these works of art only begin to obtain a wide appreciation when they are on the verge of being destroyed'.

social history of the families who commissioned and directed the work and who actually lived – in most cases, still live – in them. For while the principal rooms of many of the great houses in England and Wales were built primarily for 'state and parade', they were (and are) still essentially family homes.

The architectural history of great houses in England and Wales stretches back to the feudal fortress of the Middle Ages, built for purposes of defence rather than aesthetics. As this book is essentially about houses rather than castles, however, we have restricted ourselves to only a couple of medieval castles by way of example – Alnwick and Powis – and even they are most notable for later remodellings: Tudor and 17th-century at Powis and 18th- and 19th-century at Alnwick.

The next stage in the development of the great house was the medieval manor house, with their Great Halls used for eating and business, their solars for retiring and, often, their gatehouses and moats for defence. Haddon, which was actually never fortified, and Penshurst are outstanding examples of this type.

From the end of the 15th century, the Tudor monarchy gave England an internal peace and security such as she had never previously enjoyed, and the great houses of this period were, for the first time, universally unfortified. Instead of sheltering behind castle walls, the Tudor landowners lived in pleasant and civilized houses with large windows overlooking garden and park and the surrounding countryside.

Being so prosperous, the Tudor landowners built themselves many new country houses. These were influenced by the splendours of the Renaissance, which, broadly speaking, reached England from Italy by way of northern Europe. Although the Gothic tradition still remained powerful, the new style of architecture took note of symmetry and ornament, even – as the 16th century proceeded – of 'Classical' touches. Brick took the place

RIGHT
The elaborate Elizabeth Saloon at Belvoir Castle is named after the castle's prime mover, Elizabeth, wife of the 5th Duke of Rutland. Her statue by M.C. Wyatt is seen in the detail, and (mirrored) standing over the highly Frenchified room. The carpet is Aubusson, the panelling partly genuine Louis XV.

of timber and supplemented masonry; the use of glass for windows flourished. The English Renaissance came into full bloom during the reign of Queen Elizabeth. Romance, in its most extravagant and ostentatious form, now took the upper hand. Longleat, Burghley and Hardwick are outstanding examples included in this book.

The early 17th century saw the aristocracy achieve a high pitch of civilization, epitomized by Van Dyck's portraits in the Double Cube Room at Wilton House of the family of the 4th Earl of Pembroke, the patron of Inigo Jones, who was chiefly responsible for introducing the Classical style of the Italian Andrea Palladio into English architecture. However, it was to take nearly a century to really catch on; the style of the two great Jacobean houses in this book, Knole and Blickling, harks back more to the Elizabethan age.

Haddon Hall: The elaborately carved doorway from the Long Gallery to the Anteroom of the State Bedroom.

The late Stuart age was notable for a Dutch style of Classicism, and this is reflected in the architecture of Tredegar House in Wales. Towards the end of the 17th century, the flamboyant Baroque style was in the ascendant in such great English houses as Chatsworth, Petworth and Boughton.

The early 18th century was the golden age of the great house, not only in architectural terms but in patronage of the arts and the perfection of country house life. First came John Vanbrugh's Baroque magnificence at Castle Howard, Blenheim and Grimsthorpe. Then, in the age of Whig supremacy, came a series of great Palladian houses including Houghton, Holkham and Woburn. These 18th-century palaces, which acquired the nature of local courts, were filled with works of art collected on their owners' Grand Tours, furnished and decorated by the likes of William Kent, and set in picturesque landscapes by 'Capability' Brown – which almost invariably involved sweeping away the old formal gardens.

In the second half of the 18th century, the grandiose and austere Roman manner of the great house gave way to a most restrained and delicate interpretation of the Classical ideal. Inspired by the refreshingly feminine detail exposed in archaeological excavations of the time at Pompeii and elsewhere, the brilliant young Scot, Robert Adam, brought a new elegance to English architecture on the grand scale. Adam's genius is well represented in the pages that follow by such great Georgian houses as Kedleston, Harewood and Syon, where the decoration and furniture are all of a piece, forming exquisite ensembles.

The late Georgian age also saw the stirrings of a Gothic revival. James Wyatt, formerly a neo-Classicist, switched enthusiastically to this style. He was initially responsible for Belvoir Castle which developed into an example of romantic Regency medievalism. From the Victorian age we have featured the extraordinary French-inspired Waddesdon.

'Below stairs' service bells at Holkham Hall.

The decline of the great house as a power base can be traced back to the Reform Bill of 1832, which deprived the territorial magnates of their political power. But it was not until the First World War that there was a flood in the breaking-up of country houses and estates, as capital taxation began to bite chunks out of the great families' fortunes.

By the Second World War, the position seemed bleak indeed. In the austere aftermath of hostilities there was a prevailing pessimism that great houses had become 'white elephants', social anachronisms, doomed to extinction. The 1950s witnessed a constant and depressing series of demolitions.

The National Trust saved a number of houses for posterity, including several featured in this book – Blickling, Knole, Hardwick, Petworth, Powis, and more recently, Kedleston. Yet successive British governments failed to take the necessary steps to safeguard what became known as 'the National Heritage', and by the 1970s the crisis was so acute that private owners formed the Historic Houses Association to lobby for better conditions.

Previous studies of the subject have tended to stop the social history *circa* 1914 or, at a pinch, 1939, and to mourn the great days in the distance enchanted. The feeling was that country houses could never survive the passing of the resident servant. The present generation of owners, however, have shown this to be a nonsense, and much fresh air has been blown into frowsty old corridors.

From a contemporary viewpoint it has been refreshing to see how modern owners have courageously bucked the trend that such places are 'out of date'. As Evelyn Waugh observed in his preface to the revised edition of *Brideshead Revisited*, 'the English aristocracy has maintained its identity to a degree that then [1944] seemed impossible... Much of this book therefore is a panegyric preached over an empty coffin'.

We pay due tribute to the efforts of the 'stately home industry', pioneered by such showmen as the late Marquess of Bath of Longleat and the present Duke of Bedford at Woburn; as well as to the heritage lobby, in which the late Lord Howard of Henderskelfe at Castle Howard was such an expansive force. George Howard was only one of numerous modern owners not content merely to preserve or restore their great houses, but who continued to embellish and beautify them in the grand tradition of patronage and taste.

Chatsworth, for example, has never looked better than in the confident hands of the present Duke and Duchess of Devonshire. Nor has Penshurst, with the Viscount and Viscountess De L'Isle; or Burghley, thanks to Lady Victoria Leatham. The same must be said of Holkham, after the efforts of the Earl and Countess of Leicester; of Harewood, after its rejuvenation by the present Earl and Countess of Harewood; and indeed of several other great houses, not least the last in the book, Waddesdon Manor, now being given a superlative face-lift by the present Lord Rothschild.

It is the living families *in situ* that make these great houses so full of character and incident, of anecdote and humour in the Wodehousian tradition. Long may they remain there to give a human dimension to the visual glory.

ALNWICK CASTLE

NORTHUMBERLAND

FROM a distance Alnwick Castle in Northumberland is everything one expects from the great Border fortress of the Percys, hereditary Wardens of the Scottish Marches from early in the 14th century. Best seen from across the River Alne, the castle, with its spectacular fortifications, commands a natural defensive position on a rocky precipice above the river. Like Windsor, it seems a fairy-tale ideal of a medieval stronghold – even if, on closer inspection, some of the baronial flourishes date from the 19th century.

The rugged setting is enhanced by a fine park, in which the rocky crags were reduced, in the mid-18th century, to green slopes by Lancelot 'Capability' Brown. The castle still dominates the old town of Alnwick and one experiences a frisson of feudalism as one negotiates the medieval arch of Hotspur Tower – named after Harry 'Hotspur' Percy, the warrior-son of the 1st Earl of Northumberland – to be confronted with the menacing defile of the barbican.

Although traces of the original Norman castle remain, Alnwick was substantially rebuilt by the Percys in the early 14th century. The keep (the main castle) was remodelled with semicircular bastions and given an uncompromising entrance with twin octagonal towers. The Percys were to the fore in the long drawn-out Border warfare, but by the time of the 'Wizard Earl' of Northumberland in the early 17th century, their influence in the north of England was on the wane.

Later in the 17th century the male line of the Percys died out, and in 1670 Alnwick was inherited by Elizabeth, the four-year-old daughter of the 11th and last Earl of Northumberland. After brief unions with Lord Ogle and the scapegrace Thomas Thynne of Longleat (see pages 94–101), Elizabeth married, in 1682, the 6th 'Proud Duke' of Somerset. By this time Alnwick had fallen into decay, but parts of the castle were fitted-up for habitation and during the tenure of the 7th Duke of Somerset it again became a family seat.

The 7th Duke of Somerset had an only daughter, another Elizabeth who became the heiress to the great Northumbrian estates of the Percys. We are given a revealing portrait of Lady Elizabeth in the racy letters of the 18th-century observer, Horace Walpole. He described her as 'a jovial heap of contradictions... the blood of all the Percys and the Seymours swelled in her veins and in her fancy, her person was more vulgar than anything but her conversation, which was loaded indiscriminately with stories of her ancestors and her footmen... she was familiar with the mob, while stifled with diamonds.'

PRECEDING PAGES
Alnwick Castle: the great Border fortress of the Percys from across the River Alne.

RIGHT
The Music Room (originally Robert Adam's saloon), as done over in the Italian taste by Salvin in the 1850s, with the help of Commendatore Luigi Canina and teams of Italian craftsmen. The chimneypiece was carved by Nucci in Rome.

LEFT
A smiling Ceres, herself flanked by the fruits of the earth, beside one of Alnwick's magnificent fireplaces.

LEFT
The Guard Chamber, a
vestibule to the state
rooms of the castle, leads
off from the Grand
Staircase. The pavement
of Venetian mosaic was
made in Rome; the
circular gaming table in
the centre has decorative
swags; and the frieze
incorporates scenes by
Francis Goltzenberg
from *The Ballad of
Chevy Chase*, in which
Harry Hotspur features
prominently. The marble
figures represent Justice
and Britannia.

In 1740 Lady Elizabeth married a handsome Yorkshire baronet called
Sir Hugh Smithson. The ambitious Smithson provoked much hilarity by
exchanging his homely surname for the historic handle of Percy. Feeling that
his new position deserved appropriate recognition, he also solicited the Most
Noble Order of the Garter – 'the first Smithson to have it' as King George
II is said to have unkindly remarked – and, eventually, in 1766 he was created
Duke of Northumberland.

Although it is easy enough to make fun of Duke Hugh and Duchess
Elizabeth – whose full-length portraits by Sir Joshua Reynolds still dominate the Dining Room at Alnwick – they did have the taste and confidence
to commission the brilliant Scottish architect Robert Adam to remodel the
castle. The Duchess had a passion for Gothic, and Adam interpreted his clients'
wishes with a free treatment of 'Georgian Gothic' that was to be largely swept
away in the 19th century in favour of a more 'Baronial' style.

When Sir Walter Scott visited Alnwick early in the 19th century that great burnisher of medievalism observed that what the castle lacked was a central feature in the shape of a high tower to dominate the others. Sir Walter's suggestion was eventually followed up by the 4th ('Building') Duke – a former naval officer, a scholar, traveller and perfectionist with a 'playful disposition' – who also went a great deal further, to create what must rank as one of the most remarkable Victorian interiors in England.

As his architect the Building Duke employed Anthony Salvin, originally a pupil of John Nash. Salvin added a chapel, the Prudhoe Tower, the north terrace (which gives a majestic view of Adam's bridge across the Alne) and a massive arcade that more than holds its own against the genuine medieval architecture. Nonetheless, close up, the exterior of the domestic quarters of Alnwick Castle may strike the modern visitor as slightly disappointing after the nobility of the distant prospect. Somehow it seems a little compact for a ducal seat.

This, though, is to reckon without the wonders Salvin ingeniously contrived within the cramped shell. The sensational surprise at Alnwick is that the interior of the castle resembles a High Renaissance palace. This contrast between a feudal exterior and a sophisticated treasure house inside was a deliberate policy of the Building Duke. He wanted Alnwick to emulate the palaces he had seen in Italy: ruggedness without, polish within. To those who complained about the insertion of such lavish interiors within a medieval fortress the playful Duke replied: 'Would you wish us only to sit on benches upon a floor strewn with rushes?'

The Duke employed Italian decorators to supervise the local craftsmen who carried out the work. With their exotically coffered ceilings, damask wall-hangings and monumental chimneypieces, the series of sumptuous rooms provide a fitting background for the Northumberland art collection. The Anteroom, for instance, contains three parts of *The Visitation* (a fresco by Sebastiano del Piombo), an *Ecce Homo* by Tintoretto and no fewer than three Titians. In the Music Room are paintings by Canaletto of Alnwick and Northumberland House, the last of the great palaces that used to line the banks of the River Thames upstream from Westminster.

ABOVE
An unusual view of the castle, looking down from the town of Alnwick.

LEFT
View from the courtyard of the castle.

PRECEDING PAGES
The Library in the Prudhoe Tower at Alnwick, built by the 4th Duke of Northumberland in 1854. The two tiers of bookcases (oak, inlaid with maple) were designed by Commendatore Canina's assistant, Giovanni Montiroli.

In the Red Drawing Room at Alnwick can be found an amazing pair of French ebony cabinets, made by Domenico Cucci at the Gobelins factory in 1683 and incorporating Florentine *pietre dure*. In the Dining Room a special treat is provided by two Meissen dinner services. The family portraits extend from works by Sir Anthony Van Dyck to those of the present day. The 10th Duke of Northumberland, who died in 1988, is depicted appropriately in fox-hunting attire with Alnwick in the background.

Elizabeth Duchess of Northumberland, the 10th Duke's widow, was the former Lady Elizabeth Montagu Douglas Scott, elder daughter of the 8th Duke of Buccleuch. Her marriage in 1946 to the 10th Duke of Northumberland united the Percys and the Douglases who had, for so long in the Border warfare of the Middle Ages, been hereditary enemies. Their second son, Ralph, is now the 12th Duke of Northumberland and still lives at Alnwick. Part of the castle is let as municipal offices and one of the towers is devoted to a militia museum and armoury. The Millennium project at Alnwick is an amazing restoration of the Italian Gardens by the Belgian designer Jaques Wirtz, with water being the principal feature. It promises to be a sensational addition to Alnwick's attractions – and will be open to the public to view during its construction and evolution.

HADDON HALL

DERBYSHIRE

NOTHING could have been so sensitively done as the scholarly renovation of Haddon Hall in Derbyshire, carried out by the 9th Duke of Rutland between 1912 and 1927. The early 20th-century reverence for old manor houses, tapestries, simple wooden furniture and carving, not to mention old-fashioned roses in terraced gardens, infuses Haddon with a significant part of its charm.

And nothing captures the mood so well as Rex Whistler's idealized picture of Haddon, painted in 1933 and hung above the fireplace in the Long Gallery. The 9th Duke stands, gun over his shoulder, his dogs and his eldest son (the 10th Duke, father of the present owner, Lord Edward Manners) at his feet, and surveys what appears to be a little Gothic city set in a medieval tapestry. What could be more romantic than this vision of grey walls, battlements, towers and courtyards, perched on a spur above the River Wye?

For was it not in this very room, the Long Gallery, that Dorothy Vernon, daughter of Sir George Vernon of Haddon (the 'King of the Peak'), slipped away from her sister's wedding to elope with her lover? This swain, Sir John Manners, was, so the story goes, waiting with horses on the bridge below, at the bottom of the 76 dry-stone steps. Well, possibly; or rather possibly not. The steps, for instance, down which Dorothy is supposed to have fled, were not actually built until about a century after the alleged elopement. The elopement yarn appears to be a 19th-century fabrication to add to Haddon's air of romance. In any event, it was this marriage that brought Haddon into the Manners family in the 1560s, and they own it to this day.

For their part, the Vernons had been at Haddon since the 12th century. Yet the battlements are actually a picturesque feature of the late Middle Ages, for the house was never fortified. Indeed, it is one of the best examples of the great medieval houses that were never castles.

Haddon had assumed its present form in the late 14th century, when its two courts were bisected by the Great Hall. Sir John Manners, Dorothy Vernon's husband, gave the Long Gallery its haunting, silvery-grey panelling. Sir George Manners, their son, altered and re-roofed the chapel; and his son, John, who inherited the Earldom of Rutland in 1641, laid out much of the gardens.

Subsequently, though, the Earls and (from 1703) Dukes of Rutland principally based themselves at their Leicestershire seat of Belvoir (see pages 220–27) and Haddon fell into a long sleep.

'A gloomy and solemn silence pervades its neglected apartments', noted Rhodes in his *Peak Scenery* (1819), 'and the bat and the owl are alone among the inmates of its remaining splendour.' In all fairness, it should be said that Haddon was not altogether neglected and it can only be regarded as a blessing that the medieval house avoided the unwelcome attentions of 18th- and 19th-century 'improvers'. The happy consequence is that today Haddon seems untouched by time since the 17th century.

PRECEDING PAGES
The Banqueting Hall, erected *circa* 1370 by Sir Richard de Vernon. The screen (left foreground) is *circa* 1450; the gallery and panelling *circa* 1600; the roof-timbering is a splendid reconstruction of the 1920s for the 9th Duke of Rutland by Sir Harold Brakespeare.

RIGHT
The alcove of the Dining Room, with its carved medallions, variously said to depict Henry VII and his Queen, Elizabeth of York, or Sir George and Lady Vernon.

LEFT
The Chapel, with its medieval wall paintings, 17th-century woodwork and poignant marble effigy of Lord Haddon, carved from a model made by his mother, Violet Duchess of Rutland, in the 1890s.

From the moment one passes under the gateway at the top of the very steep uphill drive, it is difficult not to be bewitched by Haddon's spell. The sight of the deeply concave steps, worn away by generation after generation of feet, is enough to give the visitor a flavour of antiquity. As the heavy gatehouse door shuts behind you, you feel trapped in a time warp.

There, up some more eroded steps, is the enclosed lower courtyard: an apparently drunken assortment of buildings and levels held together by a labyrinthine network of squinches. The Chapel is adorned with medieval wall-paintings and a 'three-decker' pulpit in mellow early 17th-century woodwork. The west wall features three ghoulish skeletons, pointing to the medieval moral that all earthly possessions are mere vanity. The most haunting item in the chapel, however, is the 1890s effigy, in luscious white marble, of Lord Haddon, the 9th Duke of Rutland's elder brother, who died aged nine. It was carved from a model by his mother, Violet Duchess of Rutland.

Violet and her husband, the 8th Duke of Rutland, took to spending the summer months away from Belvoir in a house near Haddon. Their youngest daughter, Lady Diana Cooper, recalled how the family would go over to 'empty Haddon Hall most afternoons for water-colour sketching and gardening'. It was these visits that kindled a passionate love of Haddon in her surviving brother, John, who resolved to restore the sleeping beauty.

So successful were his efforts that today it is difficult, if not impossible, to tell which part of Haddon is original and which is a 20th-century restoration. The Banqueting Hall is the oldest room in the house where the original structure is still substantially intact. The walls, the doorways at either end, the windows and possibly also the stone floor are as Sir

The Long Gallery at Haddon: one of the great English interiors, a silvery-grey vision 110 feet long by 17 feet broad.

Richard Vernon built them *circa* 1370, though the oak screen is mid-15th century. No less impressive is the oak ceiling, which was erected in the 1920s to the design of Sir Harold Brakespeare.

Haddon's most delectable interior is, of course, the Long Gallery. This wonderfully airy room (bitterly cold in winter) is 110 feet long by 17 feet broad and illuminated by a wall of windows. Even that inveterate grumbler Horace Walpole was impressed: he pronounced the Long Gallery 'the only good room'.

When the 9th Duke of Rutland came to restore the Long Gallery he found that it needed less work than most of the other rooms. He was careful to preserve the curious bulging of the leaded windows, which produces such a magical effect when viewed from the terraced gardens outside. Here, in short, is the most romantic house in England.

RIGHT
'Childe Roland to the Dark Tower came…': the entrance in the north-west tower.

BELOW
A distant view of the most romantic house in England: like a little Gothic city set in a medieval tapestry.

POWIS CASTLE

POWYS

THE ROSE-RED castle of Powis on the Welsh side of the Marches, perched high above spectacular terrace gardens, is the closest approximation you could hope to find in reality to match the fiction of P.G. Wodehouse's idyllic Blandings Castle. Seen on a balmy summer's day, Powis, with its magnificent gardens, seems positively paradisial.

Yet its history has been turbulent. Its position on top of a rocky limestone outcrop above the Severn Valley was clearly chosen for strategic purposes; rock provided a natural defence and on the other three sides a moat was dug and earthworks raised. The present building dates back to at least *circa* 1200. It follows the Norman plan of a strong keep, and a large inner bailey (the entrance courtyard), hedged by a massive curtain wall. In the Middle Ages Powis – or Poole Castle as it was then known – was something of a shuttlecock in the Border warfare of the Welsh Marches. Eventually, in 1587, it was acquired by Sir Edward Herbert, second son of William Herbert, 1st Earl of Pembroke, a powerful figure under the Tudors to whom King Henry VIII granted the Abbey of Wilton in Wiltshire (see pages 76–85).

Between 1587 and 1595 Sir Edward Herbert extensively remodelled the interior of the old Marcher castle. Only one of his interiors survives, the Long Gallery (completed in 1593), but it is surely the finest in the house. Unusually, it is shaped in the form of the letter T, which causes a divertingly irregular play of light. Whereas the gorgeously elaborate plasterwork, the colourful heraldry, the chimneypieces, the elm floor and the delightfully dotty doorcase are all contemporary with Sir Edward's remodelling, the *trompe-l'oeil* painted wainscot presumably dates from the early 17th century.

During the Civil War Powis was captured by Parliamentary troops, who destroyed the western gateway. Later in the 17th century, however, the

PRECEDING PAGES
Powis Castle above its
magnificent terraces.

BELOW
The west front, with its forecourt
dominated by the lead statue of Fame
borne aloft by the winged horse Pegasus.
The sculpture was signed by Andries
Carpentiere (alias Andrew Carpenter), a
pupil of John van Nost, *circa* 1705; it was
derived from the marble group made by
Antoine Coysevox for Louis XIV's palace
at Marly.

RIGHT
The Grand Staircase,
attributed to Captain
William Winde. The walls,
'painted in the pompous
stile of King William's time'
(as one later critic put it),
were decorated in 1705 by
Verrio's pupil, Gerard
Lanscroon.

castle enjoyed a brief golden age under the flamboyant Marquess of Powis, who transformed the old castle into the seat of a great nobleman. In the 1660s he created an astonishing gilt-encrusted State Bedroom, the only one of its kind in Britain, where a balustrade rails off the bed alcove from the rest of the room. The reason for this was rooted in a Versailles-style ritual, whereby only the highest of the high were allowed into the vicinity of the bed.

Another of the Marquess of Powis's interiors which certainly added to that 'stile and dignity' was the Grand Staircase leading up to the state rooms on the first floor. The staircase has crisply carved woodwork and a painted ceiling by Antonio Verrio. The ceiling, adapted from Veronese's *Apotheosis of Venice*, is thought to represent the coronation of King Charles II's Queen, Catherine of Braganza.

The Marquess of Powis's architect at Powis is generally thought to have been Captain William Winde (of Buckingham House fame), a gentleman-practitioner who is on record as having designed Lord Powis's London house in Lincoln's Inn Fields. Winde's hand also appears evident in the layout of the terraces at Powis (he is known to have constructed similar features at Cliveden on the River Thames), though a Frenchman called Adrian Duval has some significant entries in the Powis archives.

After the death in exile in France of the Jacobite Lord Powis, the castle suffered further vicissitudes, though oddly enough, the 2nd Marquess of

The Clive Museum at Powis, ingeniously devised by the designer Alec Cobbe in the 'Hindoo' or 'Indo-Gothic' style of the 19th century to show off the family's exotic treasures of the Raj.

Powis was apparently able to continue building the terraces until the estates were returned to him in 1722. Later in the 18th century Powis passed to a Protestant kinsman, Henry Herbert, who was given a new Earldom of Powis. Initially he preferred to stay on at his place in Shropshire, Oakly Park. However, under aesthetic bullying from Lord Lyttelton (who reckoned that 'about £3,000 laid out upon Powis Castle would make it the most august place in the Kingdom') and financial pressure caused by the gambling of his wife, Henry settled at Powis Castle and sold Oakly to his friend, Clive of India.

Henry's bachelor son, who seems to have taken after his mother, was happiest, according to the acidulous diarist John Byng, indulging 'in the prodigalities of London and in driving high phaetons up St James's Street'. Yet he did commission the architect Thomas Pritchard to design a new Ballroom at Powis and brought back the classical marbles and vast Florentine table in the Long Gallery from his Grand Tour, when he also sat to Pompeo Batoni in Rome. Byng, though, was not won over. Such treasures, he observed sarcastically in *A Tour to North Wales* (1793), 'must add much to the comforts of the castle, in which there is not one carpet, not one bed fit to sleep in, nor, probably one hogshead of wine!! What abominable folly is all this? I should exchange the Caesars for some comforts; and the inlaid Roman table should go towards the purchase of a good English dining table'.

On the death of the bachelor Lord Powis, the castle went to his nephew, Edward Clive, a grandson of Clive of India, who was himself created Earl of Powis (the third creation) on the strength of his son's inheritance, and his son changed the family name from Clive to Herbert. The Clive connection with Powis is, however, far from forgotten, and there is an imaginative Clive Museum at the castle in the old billiard room (next to Pritchard's Ballroom in the detached wing of the castle), devoted to Indian treasures. These include objects picked up not only by the effective founder of the British Raj, but also by his son, the 2nd Lord Clive and 1st Earl of Powis, who was himself Governor of Madras.

The display cases, cleverly tricked up by the brilliant designer Alec Cobbe in an amusing evocation of the early 19th-century architectural style known as 'Hindoo' or 'Indo-Gothic', contain such items as a solid gold tiger's head encrusted with emeralds and rubies from the throne of Tipu Sahib, bejewelled hookahs and weapons, ivory, jades and silks. These exotica add greatly to the treasures of Powis, which are in themselves by no means negligible. They include a noble view of the River Adige by Bellotto; Isaac Oliver's exquisite miniature of the philosopher Lord Herbert of Cherbury in repose; and numerous other portraits, among them Nathaniel Dance's study of Clive of India.

Early in the 20th century, the 4th Earl of Powis brought in the architect G.F. Bodley to carry out various improvements in the 'Jacobethan' style. The 4th Earl lost a son in the First World War, and another in the Second, after which he bequeathed the castle and its gardens to the National Trust (with private apartments for his successors).

In 1929 he had also lost his wife Violet, otherwise Lady Darcy de Knayth in her own right, in a motor-car accident. Before her death Violet had set about transforming 'a poor and meagre garden', as she put it in her journal, into 'one of the most beautiful if not the most beautiful in England and Wales'.

The figure of Pan on the Aviary Terrace, looking out across the Welsh Marches.

PENSHURST PLACE

KENT

THE FIRST sight of Penshurst, as one breasts a wooded hill plunging down into a seemingly untouched English village, is almost overpowering. There it is, a vision of warm, mellow browns, reds and greens, weathered sandstone, brick and yew, nestling unassertively in the still-rural Kent countryside.

It is hard to think of a great house in England and Wales that has a more potent aura than Penshurst, the seat of the Sidney family from 1552 to the present day. 'Thou are not Penshurst, built to envious show', wrote Ben Jonson in 1620, 'but standst an ancient pile.' This 'ancient pile', you feel, encapsulates the history of England. The precise, and complex, architectural chronicle of the assorted towers, halls and galleries, and the catalogue of the house's treasures – splendid as they undoubtedly are – signify little. It is the *genius loci* of Penshurst which is so overwhelming.

The gardens are as old and as remarkable as the house. They date from the 14th century and retain the formal Elizabethan framework now so seldom found at other great houses, where 18th-century 'improvers' such as 'Capability' Brown have swept away the old structures. Today some 11 acres of gardens are criss-crossed by a mile of yew hedge so as to form an enchanting series of small 'rooms' out of doors.

Penshurst must surely rate as the best cared-for formal garden in Britain. Much of the credit should go to the late Viscount De L'Isle, a former Governor-General of Australia, who won the Victoria Cross at Anzio during the Second World War. 'Bill' De L'Isle carried out a thoroughgoing restoration of Penshurst and its gardens over 45 years until his death in 1991. He added such attractive new features as the Nut Garden, the Magnolia Garden and the Grey Garden (all designed by John Codrington), as well as the ingeniously coloured Union Flag Garden.

Lord De L'Isle's son Philip, the present Viscount, and his wife Isobel are carrying on the good work. The live-wire Lady De L'Isle has taken special responsibility for the gardens and contents of Penshurst; her knowledgeable enthusiasm for the place as a living entity, and above all as a family home, rather than as a museum, is most engaging. The park is also currently being restored.

A tour of the house has to begin in the Great or Barons Hall, a breathtaking 14th-century structure in a perfect state of preservation, with a massive, 60-foot-high chestnut roof, pinkish tiled floor, original hearth and 20-foot-long trestle tables. This is, quite simply, one of the great house interiors of the world.

It was built in the late 1330s by Sir John Pulteney, a prominent merchant in the City of London who was four times Lord Mayor. Subsequently, King Henry V's brother, John Duke of Bedford, added a second hall in the 15th century – a somewhat awkwardly angled addition. Yet to criticize the architectural composition of Penshurst is beside the point: the way it has grown in a distinctly haphazard fashion is an essential part of its charm.

PRECEDING PAGES
The 14th-century Barons Hall at Penshurst: one of the great interiors of the world, with a 60-foot-high chestnut roof in a perfect state of preservation.

RIGHT
Looking across the snowy courtyard to the chapel.

LEFT
One of Penshurst's many striking gargoyles.

In the early 16th century Penshurst passed to the Staffords, Dukes of Buckingham, the third of whom, the 'Proud Duke' of Buckingham, entertained King Henry VIII here in 1519. The jollifications laid on for the King cost some £2,500, and aroused uneasy suspicions in the piggy eyes of Henry who saw his host as a threat. Buckingham was arrested on a trumped-up charge of treason and beheaded; his forfeited estates duly came to the Crown.

Penshurst remained Crown property until 1552 when the boy-king Edward VI decided to reward Sir William Sidney, his tutor and the steward of his household, with the gift of the house and estate. Sir William's son, Henry, was the young King's closest friend and he went on to become a faithful servant of Queen Elizabeth I. Although Sir Henry, who was Lord Deputy in Ireland, did not enjoy great riches – in 1583 he complained

that he had not 'so much land as would graze a mutton' – he managed to make some important improvements to Penshurst without upsetting its medieval character. Among his remodelling work, he linked the Great Hall with a new range and gatehouse to the north and introduced an arcade with Tuscan columns – a remarkable novelty for 1579 and perhaps the earliest Classical loggia in England.

Sir Henry's eldest son was the legendary Sir Philip Sidney, praised by the antiquary William Camden as 'the great glory of his family, the great hope of mankind, the most lively pattern of virtue, and the glory of the world'. As well as poetry, Sir Philip Sidney wrote the prose romance *Arcadia*, dedicated to his sister Mary Countess of Pembroke, who helped make Wilton (see pages 76–85) 'an academie as well as a palace'. Sidney's description of the great house in *Arcadia*, though, is thought to have been based on Penshurst; certainly it captures the spirit of the 'ancient pile':

> The house itself was built of fair and strong stone not,
> affecting so much any extraordinary kind of fineness as
> an honourable representing of a firm stateliness...
> the consideration of the exceeding lastingness made the
> eyes believe it was exceedingly beautiful.

On Sir Philip's death at the Battle of Zutphen, Penshurst was inherited by his younger brother Robert, who was created Earl of Leicester early in the 17th century. Robert added the Long Gallery, which, lit by mullioned windows and elaborately panelled in oak, makes a fine setting for the Sidney family portraits. The 2nd Earl of Leicester collected a celebrated library – sold in the 18th century by the erratic 7th (and last) Earl of Leicester, whose wife was notorious for 'entertaining young men in rustic snuggeries and attending country dances'.

The 7th Earl's niece, Elizabeth, married William Perry and there is a hilarious conversation piece of them and their brood in the Queen Elizabeth Room at Penshurst. Perry looks a prize ass: smug, stout and supremely self-satisfied. In the scramble for Penshurst following the death of his wife's uncle in 1737, he managed to get his chubby paws on the place and set about a disastrous programme of 'Georgianization'. His scheme was inspired by 'the great window in ye baths of Pisa in Italy'. 'This is ye actual plan', he proudly

The panelled Long Gallery, lit from three sides by mullioned windows, dates from 1599 to 1607.

Penshurst: the north and west fronts.

declared, 'given me by ye architect himself on the spot. I intend it for the upper hall at Penshurst.' Fortunately, before he could wreck Penshurst altogether, Perry was certified a lunatic and clapped in an asylum.

In 1838 a guidebook compiler pleaded with the 'tasteful' Mr Perry's great-grandson, the 1st Lord De L'Isle and Dudley to remove his great-grandfather's 'monstrosities'. He duly began a sympathetic restoration of Penshurst, carried on by his son and grandson, the 1st and 2nd Lords De L'Isle. The 1st Lord added the stable wing in 1834 and the 2nd Lord brought in the architect George Devey virtually to rebuild the range built by the Duke of Buckingham in the 16th century.

Gradually, too, Perry's 'monstrosities' were removed. Out came the sash windows and in the 1920s Algy, the bachelor 4th Lord De L'Isle, restored the Long Gallery, removing Perry's Venetian window and raising the floor which Perry had lowered.

During the Second World War Penshurst was badly damaged by German flying bombs, or 'doodlebugs' as they were called. Back from his gallant service, the new Lord De L'Isle (who was to be advanced to a Viscountcy in 1956) was faced with a burdensome inheritance. Yet he set determinedly to work and by 1947 had the house ready for opening to the public.

Once more the *dernier cri* in medieval romance, Penshurst remains a popular showplace for visitors, with its rambling old buildings, *objets d'art* and tapestries, and geometric gardens. In addition to these attractions there is also a toy museum, adventure playground, nature and farm trails, with enough rare breeds of domestic animals to delight P.G. Wodehouse's Earl of Emsworth, who was portrayed here by Sir Ralph Richardson when BBC Television used Penshurst as the location for their *Blandings Castle* series in the 1960s.

SYON HOUSE

MIDDLESEX

ONE OF the joys of a walk in the Royal Botanical Gardens at Kew in Surrey is the climax of the central avenue, where the gardens meet the River Thames. There you can stop and sit on a bench to survey the prospect across the river to Middlesex. It is an unexpected sight amid the urban sprawl of Greater London: a nobleman's park adorned by the stately pile of Syon House, still the seat – or one of them – of the Duke of Northumberland.

Yet for all its air of castellated grandeur and its Percy lion in pride of place, the exterior of Syon, on closer inspection, is not all that remarkable. However, it ranks among the most illustrious buildings in England and Wales on account of its superb interiors, created by Robert Adam in the 1760s. As Sir John Betjeman observed, 'You'd never guess that battlemented house contained such wonders as there are inside it'.

Adam's patrons were the Earl and Countess of Northumberland (the former Sir Hugh Smithson and Lady Elizabeth Seymour, who took the name of Percy and ended up as Duke and Duchess of Northumberland), for whom Adam had also worked at Alnwick Castle in Northumberland (see pages 12–21). The grandiloquent Hugh and Elizabeth found Syon 'ruinous and inconvenient', and commissioned 'Capability' Brown to landscape the rather flat riverside park while Adam set about transforming the interiors of the old rectangular building.

The original monastery here had been rebuilt in the late 1540s by the Duke of Somerset, Protector of the Realm during the short reign of the boy-king Edward VI. Later in the 16th century Syon passed to the Percys, Earls of Northumberland, the 9th of whom, Henry (the 'Wizard Earl'), carried out another rebuilding early in the 17th century. Further alterations and improvements were made to Syon by the 'Proud' 6th Duke of

Somerset at the end of the 17th century. He had come into the Percy property by marrying the heiress of the 11th Earl of Northumberland, Lady Elizabeth Percy, widow of the murdered Thomas Thynne of Longleat (see pages 94–101). On the whole, though, the Proud Duke preferred to spend his time at his palatial country seat of Petworth (see pages 150–55) rather than at Syon.

Even so, it is hard to imagine that Syon was quite so 'ruinous' as his granddaughter, Elizabeth Duchess of Northumberland, made out. From the ducal viewpoint of her and her husband Hugh, however, it was clearly 'inconvenient', being built round a courtyard. When Adam arrived in 1762, still fresh from his Grand Tour, the south range contained state rooms, the north family rooms, the west a Long Gallery and the east a Great Hall. The plan was for Adam to remodel and redecorate the entire interior, and, for good measure, to put a ballroom in the courtyard. In the event, funds only permitted the young Scotsman to reach about halfway round. Nonetheless, many judges would consider that the rooms Adam did complete at Syon rank among his very finest.

The Great Hall, furnished with statues like a Roman atrium, is two storeys high with a black and white marble floor and a subtle combination of colours on the walls. The decorative stucco work is by Joseph Rose. Adam was faced with the problem of uneven floor levels, but cleverly overcame it by devising steps and a screen of Doric columns. In front of the steps leading to the Anteroom broods a bronze of *The Dying Gaul*, cast in Rome by Valadier and bought by the Duchess of Northumberland in 1773 for £300.

By contrast with the cool grandeur of the Great Hall, the Anteroom is a riot of gold and marble – including some genuine Roman marble columns dredged up from the River Tiber and brought to Syon in 1765. Adam took a special interest in contemporary archaeological discoveries and drew on the latest scholarship to show that Classical decoration could be warm and colourful rather than merely cold and monumental. The result is a glorious feeling of lavish luxury.

The Red Drawing Room takes its name from the original and still-sumptuous Spitalfields silk with which it is decorated. Adam effectively designed the Red Drawing Room only as a prelude to what he saw as the real withdrawing, or ladies' room – the Long Gallery. This he rearranged, as he put it, 'in a style to afford variety and amusement'. It was originally the 16th-century gallery, and a long, low room – 136 feet by just 14 feet high and 14 feet wide – which must have presented Adam with considerable problems. He skilfully disguised the length by breaking the room up into sections: units of four pilasters are grouped with wide intervals, centred upon

PRECEDING PAGES
The river front of Syon House, refaced in Bath stone in the early 19th century by the 3rd Duke of Northumberland. The lion was originally at Northumberland House, Charing Cross, London.

RIGHT
The bronze of *The Dying Gaul* faces Apollo, in the apse, down Adam's Great Hall, with its noble stucco work by Joseph Rose.

ABOVE
Adam's Dining Room,
adorned with marble
copies of antique statues
from Italy.

LEFT
The opulently imperial
Anteroom, with its
columns of either ancient
verde-antique (from the
bed of the River Tiber)
or scagliola. The polished
floor is a remarkable
example of 18th-century
scagliola work. The
gilded trophies were
executed by Joseph Rose.

the three doors and two fireplaces. The eye is diverted by gilded cornices, lunettes and medallions by Francisco Zuccarelli and landscapes by Thomas Marlow. The ceiling has cross-lines which somehow expand the width of the room. Last but not least the furniture in the Long Gallery is an absorbing mixture of Adam's own designs and items from old Northumberland House, the family's principal town house, high upstream on the bank of the Thames at Charing Cross.

In the early 19th century the 3rd Duke of Northumberland entertained at Syon on a princely scale. He rebuilt the north side of the quadrangle of the house and refaced all the exterior in Bath stone. He also built the riding school and added one of Syon's most notable features, the Conservatory.

This amazing Roman temple in glass was designed in the 1820s by Charles Fowler, the architect responsible for the old flower market at Covent Garden. Built of gunmetal and Bath stone, it has an extraordinarily ethereal quality, as if it was constructed of spun sugar. It is said that Joseph Paxton, once the head gardener at Chatsworth, made a detailed study of this

The Long Gallery, which stretches down the length of the river front at
Syon. Ingeniously converted by Adam from an Elizabethan or Jacobean-
style Long Gallery to a library-cum-withdrawing room, it was 'finished in
a style to afford variety and amusement'. The criss-cross lines of the
ceiling have the effect of expanding the narrow room's width. Much of
the furniture was made especially for the room by Adam.

pioneering building before designing the Crystal Palace for the Great Exhibition of 1851, and that the Syon Conservatory was also the inspiration for the Palm House at Kew, across the river.

After the Second World War, in which Syon was damaged by bombs, the Conservatory was restored by the 10th Duke of Northumberland and the house was opened regularly to the public. Syon, a majestic oasis in the metropolis, has developed a wide range of attractions, including a garden centre, craft exhibitions, a butterfly house, a National Trust gift shop and a banqueting and conference centre.

Syon has also proved popular as a film location – most memorably in the 1960s film *Accident*, starring Dirk Bogarde and Michael York – a calling particularly sympathetic to the bachelor 11th Duke of Northumberland, who was a film producer. His brother, the 12th and present Duke, and his Duchess have recently created a new garden in the central courtyard designed by the Marchioness of Salisbury, as well as a wild flower meadow in the gardens. Plans are currently under way for a major restoration of the interior which promise to remind the world of the wonders of Syon.

RIGHT
The private Drawing Room of the Duke of Northumberland at Syon.

KNOLE

KENT

IT IS characteristic of the unassertively English quality of Knole that it has no grand lodge gates, no trumpets or fanfares. Indeed it is easy to miss the narrow opening between buildings on the main road in the middle of Sevenoaks which leads, unpromisingly, down a narrow hill, to a park of deep valleys, magnificent old trees and grazing deer.

It is only when you breast another steep rise that you catch a glimpse, in the distance, of an astonishing jumble of red-tiled roofs, chimney stacks and battlements. This apparition, covering some four acres in all, strikes one not so much as a house but as a medieval village or small town.

Although owned by the National Trust, Knole is still the family home of the Sackville-Wests, Lords Sackville, and no one has expressed its potent charm better than Vita Sackville-West, only child of the 3rd Lord Sackville. She loved Knole with all the passion of one, so to speak, disinherited by her sex. If she had been a boy – as, of course, she longed to be – it would have been hers. As it was, Knole ceased to be her home on her father's death in 1928.

In that year her great friend Virginia Woolf published her novel *Orlando* (recently filmed, using Knole as a location) in which Vita is clearly the model for the hero-cum-heroine transmigrating down the line of her Sackville ancestors. Knole and its singular character resonates through the story.

Vita Sackville-West herself also featured Knole in one of her own novels, *The Edwardians*, as the family seat of 'Chevron'. One balmy summer's afternoon Sebastian, the young duke in the novel, escapes from having to play host for his mother by going on the roof. Country house roofs are supremely evocative vantage points, as Evelyn Waugh showed in *Brideshead Revisited* and Alan Bennett in his spoof Great War memoir ('We climbed out on to the leads among the turrets and towers and the green copper cupola. I remember the weather vane's shrill singing in the breeze...') in *Forty Years On*; but what could be more nostalgic than:

> Acres of red-brown roof surrounded him, heraldic beasts
> carved in stone sitting at each corner of the gables.
> Across the great courtyard the flag floated red and blue
> and languid from a tower. Down in the garden, on a lawn
> of brilliant green, he could see the sprinkled figures of
> his mother's guests, some sitting under the trees, some
> strolling about; he could hear their laughter and the tap of the
> croquet mallets.

LEFT
Gables, chimneys and yews: 'No other country but England could have produced it...'

PRECEDING PAGES
Looming out of the early morning mist, Knole looks like a medieval village or small town.

Knole: 'these irregular roofs, this easy straying up the contours of the hill, these cool coloured walls, these calm gables, and dark windows mirroring the sun'.

The Sackvilles were granted Knole in 1566 by Queen Elizabeth I, a cousin of the family. The Queen's father, King Henry VIII, had appropriated the property from the Archbishop of Canterbury and greatly enlarged it. The original house had been built by Thomas Bourchier, Archbishop of Canterbury, between 1456, when he acquired the estate, and his death in 1486, when he bequeathed it to the See of Canterbury.

The first Sackville owner, Thomas, later Lord Buckhurst and the 1st Earl of Dorset, was a poet and statesman who carried out a splendid remodelling between 1603 and 1608, probably to the designs of the surveyor John Thorpe. The consequence was that Knole, with its series of enclosed courtyards, grew to be less like a house and more like a university college.

The Great Staircase, remodelled by Thomas Sackville, 1st Earl of Dorset, between 1605 and 1608 in an innovative architectural manner. It is adorned with grisaille decoration and an unusually early example of *trompe l'oeil*.

The work was carried out on a lavish scale, with craftsmen imported from Italy and even musicians brought in to form Lord Dorset's private orchestra. Many original plasterwork ceilings, marble chimneypieces, the carved wooden screen in the hall and the painted decorations of staircase and Cartoon Gallery survive from Lord Dorset's time. Luxurious as it all sounds, it is worth bearing in mind that, judging from a letter of Lord Dorset's, he only had a single basin and ewer in which to perform his daily ablutions.

The spendthrift 3rd Earl of Dorset mortgaged Knole and died in debt to the tune of £60,000. His brother, a loyal Cavalier, lost the house to the Parliamentarians during the Civil War, when most of the original pictures and furniture were dispersed. Fortunately the 6th Earl of Dorset was able to make good these losses when he inherited the contents of Copt Hall in Essex and also through his position as Lord Chamberlain to King William III. Thanks to this Lord Dorset, Knole can now boast one of the best collections anywhere of 17th-century furniture and textiles.

In the early part of the 18th century the lst Duke of Dorset added some delicious pieces of furniture designed by William Kent to Knole's already outstanding collections, and commissioned the Huguenot artist Mark Antony Hauduroy to decorate several of the rooms. Later in the 18th century, the dashing 3rd Duke of Dorset made further important acquisitions, principally through his friendships with such artists as Sir Joshua Reynolds and Thomas Gainsborough.

During the minority of the 4th Duke of Dorset (who was a schoolfriend of the poet Lord Byron at Harrow), his stepfather, Earl Whitworth, made some minor structural changes to Knole in the Gothick manner. The dukedom died out later in the 19th century and Knole passed to the West family who became Sackville-Wests and Lords Sackville. Finally, in 1946, the 4th Lord Sackville made Knole over to the National Trust. 'It was the only thing to do', wrote Vita Sackville-West, his niece, 'and as a potential inheritor of Knole I had to sign documents giving Knole away. It nearly broke my heart, putting my signature to what I couldn't help regarding as a betrayal of all the traditions of my ancestors and the house I loved.'

Yet, though Vita Sackville-West could not bear to return to Knole – she wrote the guidebook from memory – she had a deep respect and admiration for the National Trust and all it did for the salvation of country houses. Indeed it was she who was largely instrumental in finding the ideal visionary for the first appointment of a secretary to the Trust's 'country house scheme': James Lees-Milne. He aptly described Knole as 'having a perennially romantic history and seeming to be immortal'.

The Brown Gallery, part of Archbishop Bourchier's original building, was remodelled in the Jacobean style by the 1st Earl of Dorset and given a ribbed ceiling, 88 feet in length. The room is sometimes called 'the Reformers' Gallery' because of the portraits of Luther, Melanchthon and Pomeranus among the historical array. The collection of English furniture on show here is without peer.

Detail of the state bed in the Venetian Ambassador's Room, made for James II in 1688, with hangings of Genoa velvet. Its rich carving and gilding was probably by Thomas Roberts. The bed came to Knole from Whitehall via Copt Hall as one of the 6th Earl of Dorset's 'perquisites' after Queen Mary's death in 1695.

Notwithstanding the inevitable 'museumization' necessary for conservation purposes, Knole retains its magical atmosphere under National Trust ownership. The ruggedness of the exterior, in its rough Kent rag stone, in no way prepares one for the fabulous riches within. One stands in awe before its Jacobean panelling and plasterwork, the state beds and tapestries, the luscious 17th-century furniture. The greatest thrill is to see, *in situ*, in the King's Room, the set of silver looking glass, table and stands of 1676–81 which stole the show at the great 'Treasure Houses of Britain' exhibition in Washington in 1985.

It is its unchanged quality that gives Knole part of its unrivalled charm. That, and the sheer size of it: 365 rooms (one, as legend has it, for every day of the year), 52 staircases, 7 courtyards. Only the arch-cynic Horace Walpole, in the 18th century, could have been disappointed. 'The house not near so extensive', he noted, 'as I expected...'

BELOW
The Cartoon Gallery, with its copies of Raphael's cartoons, serpentine plasterwork ceiling by Dungan and spectacular marble and alabaster chimneypiece and overmantel. The full-length portrait in the centre of the back wall shows the Earl of Surrey, in a rare 16th- or early 17th-century frame.

For the last word on Knole, though, we must leave the stage to Vita Sackville-West, whose history of Knole and the Sackvilles (now reprinted in paperback by the National Trust) is a classic of the country house genre. Knole she pointed out, is:

> no mere excrescence, no alien fabrication, no startling
> stranger seen between the beeches and the oaks. No other
> country but England could have produced it, and into no
> other country would it settle with such harmony and such
> quiet... It is not an incongruity like Blenheim or Chatsworth,
> foreign to the spirit of England. It is, rather, the greater
> relation of those small manor houses which hide themselves
> away so innumerably among the counties...

GRIMSTHORPE CASTLE

LINCOLNSHIRE

GRIMSTHORPE CASTLE in Lincolnshire is surprisingly little known. This may partly be because it has only recently been opened regularly to the public, but is more likely to be on account of its situation in England's second largest, yet least appreciated county – as the eminent local historian the Reverend Henry Thorold has put it, with withering sarcasm, 'dull, flat, boring Lincolnshire, so no one comes, thank God'.

They do not know what they are missing. For Grimsthorpe is the last great country house to have benefited from the genius of Sir John Vanbrugh, architect of Castle Howard and Blenheim (see pages 168 and 176). Having been originally commissioned by the 1st Duke of Ancaster and Kesteven in 1715, 'Van' finally began work on the north front nine years later for the 2nd Duke. The plan was for Vanbrugh to rebuild the whole of the old castle, but in the event only this front was completed.

It is more than enough to make Grimsthorpe very special indeed: a serene and gracious facade, with corner towers and Doric columns, which gloriously expresses the joys of architecture. Behind the facade is Vanbrugh's masterpiece, the supremely noble, arcaded, two-storey Great Hall – 'the Vanbrugh Hall', as it is called by the present châtelaine, Lady Willoughby de Eresby, a Maid of Honour at the Queen's Coronation and 27th holder of the title.

This ancient Barony by Writ dates back to 1313, but it was not until two centuries later that the family acquired the Grimsthorpe estate. In 1516 the 10th Lord Willoughby de Eresby married Maria de Salinas, who was also Maid of Honour to a queen – in this instance, her cousin Catherine of Aragon, first wife of King Henry VIII, who granted Grimsthorpe to the bridegroom. Later in the 16th century the Willoughbys' daughter, Katherine, married the ambitious Charles Brandon, Duke of Suffolk, Henry VIII's brother-in-law, who converted the medieval castle into a commodious quadrangular house round an open courtyard, with a second courtyard to the north. After Brandon's death in 1545, Katherine married Richard Bertie. As staunch Protestants they were obliged to flee to the continent during 'Bloody Mary's' reign, and Grimsthorpe subsequently suffered from further neglect during the tenure of their son, Peregrine, a busy military campaigner immortalized in the traditional 16th-century *Ballad of the Brave Lord Willoughby*.

It was through Peregrine's marriage to Lady Mary Vere, daughter of the 16th Earl of Oxford that the family became entitled to a share in the office of Lord Great Chamberlain. This hereditary office involves responsibility for the Palace of Westminster and helps explain the presence at Grimsthorpe of various items, such as the chairs of state in the Dining Room and regal canopies over some of the beds.

PRECEDING PAGES
The Tudorish west front from across the lake.

BELOW
'The Vanbrugh Hall', a majestic, arcaded two-storey Great Hall, with its grisaille paintings of seven English kings by Sir James Thornhill.

RIGHT
The Chapel,
magnificently restored
and redecorated by the
late Countess of Ancaster
and John Fowler. The
original design is
attributed to Nicholas
Hawksmoor, though the
ceiling and pulpit show
the influence of Inigo
Jones.

The next significant architectural improvement, however, came in the late 17th century, during the time of the 3rd Earl of Lindsey who married, as his first wife, Mary Massingberd, a co-heiress of John Massingberd, treasurer of the East India Company. He commissioned a new north front in a mature Classical style, possibly by William Winde. This elegant facade was to have a short life, being replaced only a generation or so later by Vanbrugh's north front.

Vanbrugh's Great Hall within contains seven paintings in grisaille by Sir James Thornhill (who also worked with 'Van' at Blenheim – see pages 176–83) depicting the seven English kings from whom the family received

LEFT
A corner of the State
Drawing Room, showing
portraits of the 18th-
century 3rd Duke of
Ancaster and his second
wife, the former Mary
Panton. Their daughter,
Priscilla, inherited the
Barony of Willoughby
de Eresby.

RIGHT
The doorway, with its
lavish gold fish scales,
in the exotic Chinese
Drawing Room.

titles or land through the ages. The spectacular overmantel is an enlarged version of the chimneypiece in the Duchess of Marlborough's bedchamber at Blenheim. Vanbrugh died in 1726, well before his main designs for Grimsthorpe were fully executed, and it is not clear what part his right-hand man Nicholas Hawksmoor played in the proceedings. The authorship of the chapel – one of the most ravishing interiors in England, with a ceiling in the manner of Inigo Jones – is something of a mystery, though designs are recorded in the sale of Hawksmoor's effects after his death in 1736.

Early in the 19th century Grimsthorpe passed to the 2nd Lord Gwydir (and 21st Lord Willoughby de Eresby), who commissioned the architects Samuel Page and Henry Garling to remodel first the east front and then the west front. The east front was made more castle-like, with crenellations and a tower. The west front acquired a more Tudor manner.

Lord Gwydir's grandson was created Earl of Ancaster in 1892. In the 20th century the history of Grimsthorpe was primarily a tale of two Anglo-American châtelaines: first Eloise Breese from New York, wife of the 2nd Earl of Ancaster, who tended to favour dark colours and brought in the fashionable Edwardian architect Detmar Blow to install plenty of panelling; and then her daughter-in-law, 'Wissy' Astor, wife of the 3rd Earl, who was determined to bring a lighter, lived-in touch to Grimsthorpe.

After the Second World War the 3rd Earl and his wife commissioned the architect R.J. Page and the venerable stonemason A.S. Ireson of Stamford (founder of the 'Men of Stone') to carry out a thorough overhaul of Grimsthorpe. In redecorating the interior of the house the late Lady Ancaster longed for off-white simplicity – the so-called 'English Look', a style that actually had its roots in her mother Nancy Astor's native Virginia, and was later evangelized by Lady Ancaster's cousin, the redoubtable Nancy Lancaster. Mrs Lancaster, proprietor of the interior decorators Colefax & Fowler, introduced her cousin to the designer John Fowler.

So began the double act of 'Wissy' and 'Folly' (the nickname Lady Ancaster coined for him) that transformed the stately but unfocused Grimsthorpe into one of the most stylish, cheerful and understated great houses of the late 20th century. Fowler and Lady Ancaster sparked each other

ABOVE
The old south front of Grimsthorpe Castle, which Vanbrugh never got around to rebuilding.

off; as so often in creative matters, an element of tension produced the right result. For example, in the Chinese Drawing Room, Fowler wanted to repaint the ceiling in its authentically garish bright Georgian blue. Lady Ancaster preferred something more faded. 'It takes 200 years for the right colours to fade', Fowler said. 'I don't have 200 years', Lady Ancaster replied.

Fowler and Lady Ancaster must have had particular fun in restoring the enchanting Birdcage Room in King John's Tower, where the early Chinese wallpaper of the 18th century was painstakingly repaired. The partnership continued to Lady Ancaster's death in 1974. A memorial underneath the gallery in the Chapel – the *pièce de résistance* of the new work, with its subtle shades of stone wash on the woodwork – stresses that 'The restoration of this Chapel and much of this house was accomplished by her enthusiasm and generosity'.

In 1978 her widower, the 3rd Earl of Ancaster, set up the Grimsthorpe and Drummond Castle Trust to secure the future of the Heathcote-Drummond-Willoughby heritage for the nation. The Earldom expired with his own death five years later – his heir, Timothy, had disappeared at sea in the Mediterranean in 1963 – but the ancient Barony of Willoughby de Eresby was inherited by his daughter, Jane. She and the trustees open Grimsthorpe to the public on a regular basis in the summer months. It is worth going a long way, even to the depths of Lincolnshire, to see.

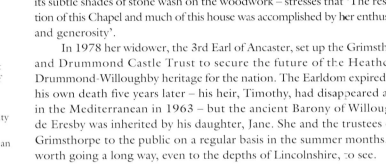

BELOW
Vanbrugh's north front at Grimsthorpe: 'out of Seaton Delaval in Northumberland by Lumley Castle in County Durham', according to the architectural historian John Harris.

WILTON HOUSE

WILTSHIRE

MANY would claim that Wilton House near Salisbury, seat of the Earls of Pembroke and Montgomery, is the most beautiful great house in England and Wales. Bearing in mind its ravishing south front with corner pavilions and a noble Venetian window, its gloriously opulent interiors such as the celebrated Double Cube Room and its exquisite Palladian bridge set in an Arcadian landscape, few could disagree.

Wilton's greatest claim to fame is its long association with the peerless English architect and pioneer of classicism, Inigo Jones. Born in 1573, the son of a London clothworker, Jones was a protégé of the 3rd Earl of Pembroke, at whose expense the budding designer travelled on the continent as a young man. The 3rd Earl was one of 'the incomparable pair of brethren', together with his brother, the 4th Earl, to whom William Shakespeare dedicated the First Folio of his plays.

Even before Jones's time, Wilton enjoyed a reputation as the nursery of the English Renaissance. The old abbey of Wilton had been granted by King Henry VIII, after the Dissolution of the Monasteries, to Sir William Herbert, 1st Earl of Pembroke, in 1542. The Pembrokes were a bastard scion of the illustrious Norman-Welsh family of Herbert, which is also represented in the female line by the Dukes of Beaufort at Badminton and the Earls of Powis at Powis (see pages 30–39).

The 1st Earl, a shrewd operator who managed to enjoy favour under four Tudor sovereigns, transformed the monastic buildings into a Tudor seat, built round a courtyard. In the Elizabethan heyday of the 2nd Earl of Pembroke and his Countess, Mary, sister of Sir Philip Sidney of Penshurst (see pages 40–49), Wilton, in the words of the local antiquary John Aubrey became 'an academie as well as a palace'.

PRECEDING PAGES
Inigo Jones's Double
Cube Room at Wilton
House: one of the most
deservedly celebrated
interiors in England. It
takes its name from the
fact that it is double the
length (60 feet long; but
30 feet wide and high)
of the adjoining room
which is a perfect 'cube'.
It was used as a dining
room in the 18th
century, though in the
19th and 20th centuries
it was both a drawing
room and ballroom. The
portraits of the Herberts
are by Van Dyck, the gilt
furniture by William
Kent and Thomas
Chippendale.

ABOVE LEFT
A view of the east front
(originally the entrance),
looking across to the
Palladian bridge, which
is on the left of the
picture.

Then, in the 1630s the 4th Earl of Pembroke carried out the Renaissance remodelling of Wilton. According to Aubrey again, it was King Charles I that 'did put Philipp Earl of Pembroke upon making this magnificent garden and grotto, and to new build that side of the house that fronts the garden, with two stately pavilions at each end, all *al Italiano*'. Work was in progress on a vast new formal garden by 1632 and on the south front by 1636. The executant responsible for both was Isaac de Caus, but, as Aubrey mentions, he had 'the advice and approbation' of Inigo Jones.

Jones liked simple geometrical measurements in his designs. Wilton boasts both a Single Cube Room (30 by 30 by 30) and a Double Cube Room (60 by 30 by 30), two of the most celebrated interiors in England and Wales. The Double Cube Room is adorned with carved swags of fruit, flowers and Classical masks, and its panelling was designed to show off a series of portraits of the Herberts by Sir Anthony Van Dyck. The splendid gilt

RIGHT
The Gothic vaulted
cloister-corridor, inserted
by James Wyatt for the
11th Earl of Pembroke.
It serves as a fine gallery
for the sculpture
collection.

ABOVE

Classical undress: detail of one of the carved figures flanking the doorway of Lord Pembroke's private drawing room.

RIGHT

The Earl of Pembroke's private drawing room.

furniture by William Kent and Thomas Chippendale, added a century later, is perfectly in keeping. In the Single Cube Room, which has a coved ceiling of arabesques, there are dado paintings of scenes from Sir Philip Sidney's prose romance *Arcadia*.

While no one doubts Jones's vital influence on the south front and state rooms at Wilton, his precise role remains unclear. Matters are complicated by the fact that the south front suffered a bad fire in 1647–8. The necessary rebuilding work and reconstruction of the interior was undertaken by John Webb, a pupil and nephew-by-marriage of Inigo Jones. By this stage Jones was an old man, but the faithful Aubrey insists that he still had a hand in the proceedings and one is inclined to believe him. By way of documentary evidence, drawings for the interior survive, dated 1649, and some of them are indeed annotated by Jones and Webb.

Jones's long connection with the Herberts and Wilton finally came to an end with his death in 1652, a couple of years after the 4th Earl's demise. Of the subsequent Lords Pembroke, the 8th Earl was a connoisseur on the grand scale, collecting antique sculpture, books, drawings and paintings and the 9th Earl, known as the 'Architect Earl', was to the fore in the Palladian movement with the Earl of Burlington and William Kent. It was this Lord Pembroke who built the beautiful bridge across the River Nadder in the park, and in the process swept away de Caus's formal garden of a century before. The Architect Earl, with the assistance of the professional designer Roger Morris, designed the bridge in 1737 on the pattern of a drawing by Andrea Palladio.

The 10th Earl of Pembroke, a military man, brought in the architect Sir William Chambers to build an arch surmounted by an equestrian statue of Marcus Aurelius. Initially, this arch was erected on top of the hill south of Wilton as an eyecatcher, but in the time of the 11th Earl of Pembroke, the architect James Wyatt brought it down so as to close the new forecourt of the house.

Wyatt played a significant part in Wilton's architectural history. He rebuilt both the west range and the north front, which became the main entrance. He created the present forecourt by giving it embattled walls and raising the ground level, and by adding two lodges on either side of Chambers's arch. The former main entrance on the east was converted into a Gothic garden hall, through which today's visitors end their tour. The architect improved the logistics of the interior by inserting a Gothic vaulted cloister-corridor within the inner courtyard, which served not only as a gallery for the 8th Earl's collection of sculpture but also as a useful passage. Wyatt wisely left the Jonesian part of the house well alone. Later generations, however, treated Wyatt's own Gothic touches with less reverence. The

15th Earl of Pembroke, who succeeded to Wilton in 1913, promptly commissioned Edmund Warre to 'unGothicize' the north side of the house.

The 15th Earl's elder son and successor, Sidney, the 16th Earl, repainted the Upper Cloisters in terracotta and grey, changing them from Wyatt's grey stucco of 1814, and also replaced Wyatt's painted wood and slate clock turret, or cupola. The 16th Earl had had a hand in the design of the new cupola and was a scholarly connoisseur in the tradition of his family.

His younger brother, David Herbert, author of an amusing memoir *Second Son*, also had aesthetic tastes and in the brothers' younger days, before the Second World War, Wilton once more became a fashionable haunt of artists and writers. One of them, Cecil Beaton, left a vivid account of Sidney's coming-of-age celebrations in 1927: 'In the gloaming the Inigo Jones facade looked its most noble with the long range of tall lighted windows... It was a grand occasion... How beautiful the night scene was! How calm and visionary'. Unfortunately Beaton's reveries proved short-lived. As he recalled in *The Wandering Years*, he was suddenly surrounded by a group of thuggish hearties and frog-marched across the lawns ('I remember my head was raised in a Guido Reni agony') before being thrown into the Nadder. 'Do you think the bugger's drowned?' he heard one of his tormentors ask in the dark.

As a memorial to Sidney Pembroke, who died in 1969, his son, the 17th and present Earl, commissioned the landscape gardener David Vicary to create a new formal garden, with a circular pool, in Wyatt's north forecourt. The present Lord Pembroke is (as Henry Herbert) a successful film and television director who has applied his cinematic expertise to presenting an in-house video documentary film of *The Lives and Times of the Earls of Pembroke*.

RIGHT
'Blow, Gabriel, blow...' A rooftop view of the idyllic landscape, set off by the Palladian bridge.

BURGHLEY HOUSE

CAMBRIDGESHIRE

THE PRE-EMINENCE of Burghley House in Northamptonshire (now dumped in Cambridgeshire by the odious boundary changes of the 1970s) as the greatest treasure house in England and Wales was illustrated by the fact that the landmark 'Treasure Houses of Britain' exhibition, held in Washington in 1985, featured no less than 38 items – far more than from any other family seat – from the Elizabethan stronghold of the Cecils.

Indeed there is so much to see at Burghley, a fairy-tale structure of towers and turrets set in one of 'Capability' Brown's finest parks, that the visitor can feel somewhat overwhelmed. There is almost too much for the visitor to take in. Fortunately the present châtelaine, Lady Victoria Leatham, youngest daughter of the 6th Marquess of Exeter, is the very model of a modern historic house curator and has rationalized the presentation of Burghley in a most impressive manner. To help focus attention on detailed aspects of the house's extraordinarily rich collections, 'Vicky' Leatham has arranged a series of exhibitions in the courtyard gallery highlighting such subjects as silver, jewels, miniatures, scientific instruments, clocks, books and oriental porcelain. Engagingly humorous and down-to-earth, Vicky Leatham is celebrated for her breezy performances on such television programmes as *The Antiques Road Show* and *Heirs and Graces*. Beneath the delightfully unstuffy manner, though, is considerable expertise: Lady Victoria is a director of Sotheby's and has a special passion for what she calls 'old pots'.

Her father set up a charitable preservation trust to own and manage Burghley before his death in 1981, and the trust appointed Lady Victoria as its curator. She has brought enormous enthusiasm and energy to the task of revitalizing a place that had rather gone to sleep, and to doing justice to the scope of its treasures. Lady Victoria has also been a pioneer in getting commercial sponsorship for restoration work. A subtle difference has been wrought by the introduction of halogen lighting, which brings out the artistry of the objects on view in sharp relief. Among the many other improvements in the showing of Burghley, the formerly cluttered Great Hall has been dramatically cleared to provide a fitting climax to the house tour.

The Great Hall, together with the kitchen, is one of the few surviving interiors of the original Elizabethan house. The Gothic hall, more than 60 feet in height, has a steep double hammer-beam roof and a soaring, Classical chimneypiece; the Kitchen has a lofty stone vault rising to a lantern (only recently rediscovered and restored), which would have served to extract smoke. The Old Kitchen in particular evokes the world of the Tudors in which the Cecil family, perhaps the best known of the so-called 'New Men' – being descended from modest gentry called Sysilt in the Welsh Marches – flourished so spectacularly.

William Cecil, the builder of Burghley, rose to become the most powerful man in England as Queen Elizabeth I's chief minister. Cecil began

PRECEDING PAGES
A fairy-tale vision reflected in the lake: Burghley House, treasure house of the Cecils.

LEFT
The Hell Staircase (recently cleaned by the conservationist Michael Cowell), where the Italian Antonio Verrio portrayed, in the early 18th century, the mouth of Hades as the gaping mouth of a cat. The walls were painted a century later by Thomas Stothard. The cantilever staircase is 1786 and of local Ketton stone. Against the wall at the bottom of the well of the staircase is an elaborate musical box by Samuel Troll *et fils* of Switzerland, *circa* 1870.

RIGHT
Verrio's masterpiece, the Heaven Room (now undergoing cleaning), painted with remarkably lifelike scenes from ancient mythology. The artist himself is depicted sitting at the forge of Cyclops (right), without his wig. The carpet is an English copy of a Savonnerie.

building Burghley of the durable local Barnack rag stone in about 1555, when there is evidence that the east and south ranges were going up. Cecil appears to have been his own architect, with a little help from an Antwerp mason called Henryk. His correspondence shows that he could supply a 'tryke' (drawing) of some detail when required.

William Cecil's devoted service to the Queen brought him great riches but no higher rank than baron as Lord Burghley. His younger son, the ambitious hunchback Robert Cecil, who succeeded his father as the Queen's minister and later served King James I, acquired the Hatfield estate in Hertfordshire at the other end of the Great North Road, and was raised to the peerage as Earl of Salisbury on the same day as his elder brother, William, was created Earl of Exeter.

The 5th Earl of Exeter was a tireless collector, spending much time on the continent picking up tapestries, statuary and furniture, as well as numerous Florentine and Venetian paintings. At home he was the patron of Jean Tijou, the iron-worker who produced the Golden Gates for the west front; Grinling Gibbons and the school of woodcarvers who emulated his work; and John Vanderbank, the tapestry weaver. Above all, he commissioned Antonio Verrio to decorate the 'George Rooms'.

This Neapolitan artist, together with his family and other hangers-on, was installed at Burghley for 11 years and lived like a prince at Lord Exeter's expense while he painted away, covering the ceilings with a fantastic array of mythological figures. Verrio's masterpiece was the Fifth George Room, or 'Heaven Room', in which both walls and ceiling are devoted to 'The Rage of Vulcan' (as related by Homer in *The Odyssey*). All the gods have come to enjoy the spectacle of the adulterous Venus and Mars, naked as nature intended, caught in Vulcan's net, while Neptune offers to take Venus as his own wife.

By way of contrast to the Heaven Room, Verrio then began work on the 'Hell Staircase', showing the vast gaping mouth of a cat and screaming souls in torment within as Death, the Grim Reaper, plies his sickle among them. Verrio only managed to finish the ceiling here, and indeed the George Rooms were by no means complete when the 5th Earl of Exeter himself succumbed to the Grim Reaper in 1700.

His great-grandson, the 9th Earl, completed the furnishing of the George Rooms and added many outstanding pictures and other objects to the collections at Burghley, including the Veronese altarpiece in the chapel and the Piranesi chimneypiece in the Second George Room. It was the 9th Earl, too, who brought in 'Capability' Brown not only to sweep away the formal gardens started by Henry Landon for the 5th Earl, but also to make various architectural changes to the house – such as tidying up the

RIGHT
The recently restored state bed in the Second George Room. Originally supplied by the London firm of Fell & Newton in 1795 for £3,000 (a vast sum of money in those days), it was reduced in size and decorated with the royal arms for Queen Victoria's visit to the house in 1844.

skyline, and adding the stable courtyard and the orangery. Lady Victoria Leatham, who refers trenchantly to 'that blasted Brown', has begun to restore the formal gardens he destroyed.

At the beginning of the 19th century, the 1st Marquess of Exeter – immortalized in Tennyson's romantic account of his humble marriage, *The Lord of Burleigh* – commissioned Thomas Stothard to complete the Hell Staircase. Stothard successfully covered the walls with more visions of dark doom and gloom: 'War', 'Intemperance' and 'Orpheus Descending to the Underworld'. In the time of the 3rd Marquess, the gossipy country-house crawler Augustus Hare wrote of Burghley: 'There is a series of state rooms, dull and oppressive, and a multitude of pictures with very fine names, almost all misnamed'.

That is not altogether an unfair description of this great house, up to its present renaissance under Lady Victoria Leatham. Today it is bursting with life and full of absorbing objects to admire – from silver fireplaces, needlework and copper utensils to the now carefully attributed art and antiques. Particularly evocative are the memorabilia connected with Lady Victoria's father, the 6th Marquess of Exeter, who as Lord Burghley carried all before him on the athletics track in the 1920s and early 1930s.

Among the many enterprising schemes pioneered by Lady Victoria and her team at Burghley are stable workshops for conservation, furniture, silver and goldsmithery, textiles and bookbinding. In the grounds, a Sculpture Garden has been established, linked to a gallery in the house selling contemporary art. In short, this joint is jumping.

RIGHT
The so-called Roman
Staircase.

LONGLEAT

WILTSHIRE

THE present Marquess of Bath commissioned an exhibition on the life and times of Henry, Lord Bath, as a memorial to his father, who died in 1992. It is also the story of Longleat 'the house he loved, and saved'. Henry Bath was the 'founding father of the stately home industry': the first owner of a great house to open it to the public on a full-blown commercial basis after the Second World War. Faced with a bill of £750,000 in death duties, he threw open the doors of Longleat in 1949 and entered enthusiastically into the then novel role of titled showman. By 1957 he was able to welcome, with a characteristic flourish, the millionth visitor.

Lord Bath deployed every tripperish magnet conceivable: a funfair, pedal boats on the mile-long lake, a putting green and tearooms. To the disapproval of his fellow peers he even allowed 'Capability' Brown's dramatically plunging park to be used for staging pop concerts – a practice subsequently copied at other great houses. It was in the 1960s when the Longleat tourist venture really took off. The circus impresario Jimmy Chipperfield suggested introducing game to roam the estate. Led by the celebrated lions, it grew into a safari park of international fame, with tigers, baboons, chimpanzees, giraffes, hippos and sea lions.

Yet the 6th Marquess of Bath deserved to be remembered for more than 'the Lions of Longleat'. He laid out a new formal garden in keeping with the house; planted extensively in the park; sat for a portrait by Graham Sutherland (wearing his familiar, tramp-inspired polka-dot tie); commissioned new furniture by John Makepeace and other works of art; added many hundreds of books to the libraries (even if he spent little time reading them); and was an inveterate collector of memorabilia: Churchilliana, Hitleriana (Lord Bath found the Führer's watercolours of particular interest) and

Thatcheriana (including 'Maggie' toilet-paper rolls and puppets and mugs from the satirical television show *Spitting Image*).

Above all, though, he kept Longleat alive as a going concern – even if, as he pointed out, the net takings from the tripper attractions failed to cover the costs of daily maintenance and repair of the great house – the first of what Sir John Summerson has called 'the Elizabethan prodigy houses'. Longleat was built in at least three stages by Sir John Thynne, an ambitious and archetypal Tudor 'New Man', who bought the old priory here in 1541 for a mere £55. Thynne was a nephew of William Thynne, Clerk-Comptroller of King Henry VIII's household, who probably insinuated him into the entourage of Edward Seymour, the future Duke of Somerset and Protector of the Realm. As 'Protector' Somerset's steward and man of business, Sir John Thynne accumulated a large fortune and also developed a passion for building. He was intimately involved in the building work for his master's houses on the Thames, at Somerset House in London and at Syon (see pages 50–57).

At his own property in Wiltshire, Thynne began by converting the modest remains of the priory into living quarters for himself and his wife, the City of London heiress Christian Gresham. In the 1550s and 1560s he gradually enlarged, extended and rebuilt his new house with stone dragged across

PRECEDING PAGES
The Great Hall, with its Mannerist chimneypiece, beamed roof (lowered late in the 17th century to fit in Bishop Ken's Library above), and screen of *circa* 1600. On the right are two of the equestrian paintings by John Wootton that fill the upper walls. Commissioned by the 2nd Viscount Weymouth (seen in the picture above the fireplace, with hand on hip), they tell the story of an orphan taken on as a stable lad at Longleat, who was killed at the age of 14 trying to separate two fighting stallions.

LEFT
Renaissance roofscape.

the combes from his own quarry at Box. The setback of a fire in 1567
only spurred Thynne on to renewed efforts.

Soon after the fire, the significant name of Robert Smythson, one of
the geniuses of English architecture who was later to work at Hardwick (see
pages 102–11), first turns up in the records of Longleat. The accounts show

that Smythson, who spent a dozen years at Longleat, carved much of the house's exterior detail, but it is difficult to apportion credit for the overall design of the building that began to take its final shape after 1572.

In any event, at the time of Thynne's death in 1580 Longleat had become a remarkable Renaissance palace, combining innovative Classical outline and detail with the English Gothic tradition. Its vast mullioned windows, allowing the light to flood in, made Longleat

ABOVE
The Red Library contains some 6,000 volumes, mainly collected by the 4th Marquess of Bath. The drawing displayed on the easel on the extreme left of the photograph is by John Singer Sargent, and shows the wife of the 5th Marquess.

the first great 'lantern house'. Here, in the words of Mark Girouard, Smythson's biographer, was 'a sudden efflorescence of splendour that ushered in the great age of Elizabethan architecture'.

Four hundred years on, the exterior remains little altered. The Baroque doorway and the statues on the balustrade (itself inspired by Somerset House, which had a decisive influence on the symmetry and Classical flavour of Longleat) were added at the end of the 17th century during the time of the 1st Viscount Weymouth. Lord Weymouth had inherited Longleat in 1682 from his dissolute cousin Thomas Thynne, known as 'Tom o' Ten Thousand', who lived at the house in extravagant style. Tom had married the heiress Lady Elizabeth Percy of Alnwick (see pages 12–21), to the fury of another fortune hunter, the Swedish Count Königsmark, who arranged for a hired thug to blast Thynne away with a blunderbuss in his coach in Pall Mall a few months later.

RIGHT
Detail of a marquetry door leading from the breakfast room into the dining room at Longleat.

In the 1690s the 1st Viscount Weymouth commissioned George London to lay out extensive formal gardens at Longleat, with parterres stretching in front of the house, clipped hedges, canals and statues. These had become run down by the 18th century, when they were removed by 'Capability' Brown. Inside the house Lord Weymouth, a High Churchman, built a chapel and gave shelter to Bishop Ken of Bath and Wells. Bishop Ken's Library, a charmingly plain and simple room of the 1690s, is still to be found above the Great Hall at Longleat.

The Elizabethan beamed roof of the Great Hall was flattened to accommodate this insertion, and the 1st Viscount Weymouth was probably also responsible for the balcony with open-work scrolls in the same room. There are still some original touches in the Great Hall such as the Mannerist chimneypiece, with two-tailed mermaids, but the 'Jacobean' panelling is most likely 19th-century work. Indeed most of the interior of Longleat is 19th-century – and none the worse for that, as it displays craftsmanship of the highest quality, first by Sir Jeffry Wyatville (of Windsor Castle fame) and then, later in the century, by John Crace.

Wyatville's patron was the 2nd Marquess of Bath. Between 1801 and 1811 the architect rebuilt the north front of Longleat; added the Elizabethan revival stables and clock tower; and radically rearranged and remodelled the interior of the main house. He inserted passages round the inner courtyard and constructed the 'Imperial' Staircase.

The grandiose decorative work by Crace in the 1870s was carried out for the diplomatist and connoisseur 4th Marquess of Bath. Keen on all things Italian, especially Venetian, this Lord Bath had Crace set mythological canvases of the Titian school into a scrolling gilt ceiling in the State Dining Room. Besides Crace and his firm, the 4th Marquess also employed George Fox in the decoration of some of the seven Italianate rooms at Longleat.

BELOW
A royal gallery in light and shade.

ABOVE
The delightful 1690s
library of Bishop Ken, to
whom the 1st Viscount
Weymouth gave shelter
at Longleat after the
'Glorious Revolution'.

An evocative memoir of life at Longleat in the mid-20th century is given in *Mercury Presides*, a volume by Henry Bath's first wife, Daphne Vivian (later Fielding). Their eldest son, Alexander, the present Marquess who has changed the spelling of the family name from Thynne to Thynn, has been busy at Longleat since the 1960s – whether painting his celebrated series of erotic murals; laying out a roof garden and a *yin-yang* garden, as well as a series of mazes; installing adventure castles for young visitors and a banqueting suite for paying guests; or encouraging Center Parcs to build a new holiday village in the woods. Lord Bath has also championed the Wessex Regionalist cause, written novels and most recently an autobiography, *Strictly Private*, which is available on his Internet website, designed, as he says, 'to attract new tourists into the fold'.

HARDWICK HALL

DERBYSHIRE

THERE was something so vivid and larger-than-life about the Tudor age that its great figures, such as King Henry VIII and Queen Elizabeth I, have projected their personalities with such strength down the centuries that they still seem to be living memories. Another Tudor Elizabeth, 'Bess of Hardwick', no less formidable in her own way, ensured her immortality through building surely the most remarkable Elizabethan house of them all, Hardwick Hall in Derbyshire.

'Hardwick Hall/More glass than wall' goes the old jingle and drivers on the motorway far below in the valley must echo the refrain when the rays of the sun strike the four storeys of huge windows. The result is a glittering wall of flame. On the more frequent cloudy days of the English Midlands, it stands silhouetted against the sky, massive and mysterious like a great galleon.

Bess's extraordinary life was intimately tied up with the building of Hardwick, which remains her memorial and monument. She was born at Hardwick in 1527, one of four daughters of John Hardwick, whose family had been settled hereabouts for at least six generations. The family seat was originally a modest manor house now subsumed by the ruins of Hardwick Old Hall.

Her father died when Bess was still an infant and she was brought up in straitened circumstances. Yet she accumulated a fortune through a progression of shrewd marriages – so shrewd as to make one mildly suspicious of her husbands' causes of death. Her second husband, Sir William Cavendish of Cavendish in Suffolk, was an immensely rich widower who had served as one of the commissioners for the Dissolution of the Monasteries. Bess persuaded him to concentrate his landholdings in Derbyshire – among the new acquisitions was the estate of Chatsworth (see pages 140–49). By the time Sir William Cavendish died, Bess, who had borne him eight children, was hitting her stride as an acquisitive and ambitious schemer with a passion for building. Next she married Sir William St Loe, a West Country landowner. And in 1567 she snapped up her fourth and most spectacular catch, the 6th Earl of Shrewsbury, Premier Earl of England and a powerful Tudor tycoon with interests in all manner of commercial concerns besides vast land-holdings.

However, the union – one might almost say merger – did not turn out well. Apart from the clash of two strong personalities, one of the flies in the ointment was the exiled Mary Queen of Scots, of whom Lord Shrewsbury was appointed custodian in 1569. The intriguing (in both senses of the word) Mary was shuffled around Lord Shrewsbury's numerous seats, much to Bess's annoyance.

In the early 1580s the marriage came apart at the seams. Bess decided to decamp to her own stronghold of Hardwick, which she had recently acquired from her bankrupt brother, James. It was as if she said 'I'll show them!' And she did.

First of all, between 1585 and 1590, when Lord Shrewsbury died, she transformed her old family home into a rambling, rather haphazardly designed mansion. Then, flush with almost limitless wealth, she decided to start all over again by building a new house only about 100 yards away. This was to be her conclusive statement: Hardwick Hall, a triumphant, symmetrical, deceptively simple expression of the English Renaissance in glass, stone, tapestry and embroidery. Her initials *ES* (Elizabeth Shrewsbury), carved repeatedly on the parapets of the six towers, shouted her ownership from the roof-tops.

The extravagant use of glass, an expensive commodity in Tudor times, was a status symbol, and Bess was in a strong position to show off in this area as one of the many assets she had inherited from Lord Shrewsbury was a glass works. Hardwick was also conveniently placed for other materials. Stone came from a quarry halfway up the drive; slate from sites on the Cavendish estates; lead from workings owned by her son William, the future 1st Earl of Devonshire; and iron from her own furnace. The enormous trees needed for floors and roofs came from her extensive woodlands, stretching to Chatsworth.

The house did not have an 'architect' as such, the term not then being in popular use, but rather what was called a 'surveyour' in the form of Robert Smythson, who had previously worked at Longleat (see pages 94–101). The symmetry of the exterior is reflected inside the house by the planning of the hall. Instead of its traditional disposition, running parallel to the front,

PRECEDING PAGES
The main staircase at Hardwick, made of local stone, leading one ever upwards.

BELOW
The chimneypiece and doorway
by Thomas Accres in the Green
Velvet Room: a symphony of
Derbyshire marbles.

we find the hall cutting straight through the centre of the house. At its west end a screen of columns supports a gallery which provides communication between the two wings of the house, while beyond this, on either side, are two staircases.

These staircases are among the most memorable features of this extraordinary house. Built from the light-coloured local stone, they have been worn by the tread of generations of Hardwick feet. As they progress ever upwards they seem to take on a life of their own. Up and up they climb until they finally reach their summits in the north and south turrets, some 80 feet from where they set out.

The High Great
Chamber, where Bess
held state. The plaster
frieze depicts the Virgin
Goddess, Diana the
Huntress. The arms of
Queen Elizabeth above
the chimneypiece feature
Bess's own monogram
interwoven with the
motto; a case
of over-identification.

En route, they stop at the first floor where Bess maintained her private suite of rooms. The splendid state apartments are on the floor above. The High Great Chamber, a wondrous affair filled with soft light and surrounded by an elaborate painted frieze celebrating Diana the Huntress, the Virgin Goddess (and by implication, Good Queen Bess), is where Bess of Hardwick dined when she was keeping state. Food was ceremoniously borne from the kitchen two floors below, and must have been stone-cold when it reached the table.

Next door is the Long Gallery to end long galleries – a superlative sight, running 166 feet from one end of the house to the other. The tapestries here were bought by Bess from the bankrupt estate of Sir Christopher Hatton, Queen Elizabeth I's Lord Chancellor. The two chimneypieces boast alabaster statues of Justice and Mercy in differently coloured marbles.

An inventory drawn up in 1601 shows that Bess filled Hardwick with treasures. Many of the items are still *in situ*, notably the tapestries, furniture and, above all, the embroideries. Hardwick's collection of late 16th- and early 17th-century embroidery is without equal. Bess herself was an expert and prolific needlewoman and presided over a hive of embroiderers – even if, legend notwithstanding, Mary Queen of Scots was not one of the team.

Bess lived on at Hardwick into the new century, finally dying in 1608. She was buried in great state at Derby. The epitaph on her tomb aptly describes her as '*aedificatrix*'.

Hardwick passed to her Cavendish descendants, who later became Dukes of Devonshire and based themselves largely at Chatsworth. Yet they far from neglected the great Elizabethan house, at least in the summer months. With all the glass, it must have been bitterly cold. The 6th ('Bachelor') Duke of Devonshire enhanced the antiquarian atmosphere at Hardwick, importing appropriate tapestries, furniture and pictures. In the 20th century an enormous amount of skilled repair work on the tapestries and embroideries was carried out by Evelyn Duchess of Devonshire, who spent her days at Hardwick after the death of her husband, the 9th Duke, in 1938. The programme of sensitive conservation has continued under Hardwick's new owner, the National Trust, which took the place over in 1956.

Symmetry in the snow.

BLICKLING HALL

NORFOLK

THAT IT was possible for the National Trust to take on Hardwick Hall, and several other great houses featured in this book (such as Powis Castle, Knole, Petworth, Kedleston and Waddesdon), was due to the vision of the 11th Marquess of Lothian, the Liberal statesman who inherited the title and the estate of Blickling in Norfolk in 1930.

As Philip Kerr, he had first made his mark in public life as private secretary to David Lloyd George, the Liberal Prime Minister who did more than anyone else to erode the supremacy of the British aristocracy. Concerned about the seepage of family seats and their contents on to the market, Lord Lothian made an historic speech in 1934 to the annual general meeting of the National Trust, which had previously only concerned itself with the protection of the landscape. He warned of the perils facing England's great houses and urged the Trust to devise a 'Country Houses Scheme' whereby, instead of being dispersed as a result of death duties, whole houses and their contents could be left to the nation intact with their estate income as an endowment.

The upshot was a Bill in Parliament, instituted in 1937, which allowed the National Trust to save country houses. Lord Lothian himself initiated the process by bequeathing Blickling to the National Trust on his death *en poste* as British Ambassador to the United States of America in 1940. Nearly 100 other country houses have followed Blickling into the Trust's care but none can displace it as a perfect representative of the English country house.

According to tradition, Blickling was the birthplace of Anne Boleyn, King Henry VIII's bewitching second queen. True or not, this legend contributes significantly to Blickling's air of romance. In 1616 the estate was

PRECEDING PAGES
Blickling: the north
front, seen in the
morning from across
the lake.

LEFT
Double vision in the
Stone Court.

bought by Sir Henry Hobart, Lord Chief Justice of the Common Pleas and one of the first Baronets created by King James I. Sir Henry set about rebuilding the old manor house in such a grandiose and expensive fashion that Blickling became one of the stateliest Jacobean seats.

　　As his architect, or 'surveyor' (as they still tended to be called), Hobart went to the top: Robert Lyminge, who had previously built Hatfield House in Hertfordshire for King James's Lord Treasurer, Robert Cecil, Earl of

LEFT
A bird's-eye view of
Blickling roof-tops.

RIGHT
The Great Staircase, with
its curious newel figures,
as redecorated in the
19th century by the 8th
Marquess of Lothian.

Salisbury, son of William Cecil, Lord Burghley (see pages 86–93). In architectural terms the two houses have obvious stylistic similarities, but Blickling's trump card over Hatfield is the variety of its elaborate plaster ceilings, carved by the stuccoist Edward Stanyon.

The ceiling in the Long Gallery is the house's chief wonder – 'a dense and intricate pattern of bands enclosing heraldic and emblematic panels. There are symbols of the five senses and some 20 emblems derived from Henry Peacham's *Minerva Britannia* (1612). One could certainly spend the best part of a day on one's back in the Long Gallery peering up at the ceiling with its charmingly chunky and naive plasterwork.

The extravagance of the building operation became rather out of hand and Sir Henry Hobart, who died in 1625, did not live to see its completion. The cruel truth is that, like Sir Nathaniel Curzon at Kedleston (see pages 212–19), he had built above his station. He lumbered a far from great family with a great house. Blickling proved a burdensome inheritance for the fairly dim line of Norfolk baronets that followed him.

Nonetheless, in the 18th century the Hobarts advanced to the Earldom of Buckinghamshire, not so much through any merit as by the charms of the 1st Earl's sister, Henrietta, the Countess of Suffolk, who was King George II's mistress. The 2nd Earl of Buckinghamshire was to be a key figure in Blickling's late 18th-century revival. It was fortunate indeed

LEFT

The State Bedroom, finished *circa* 1782. The tester and backboard of the bed are made up from a canopy of state issued to the 2nd Earl of Buckinghamshire for his Russian embassy. The royal arms on the coverlet, though, are those of Queen Anne, and must have come from an earlier canopy. The Axminster carpet was made for the room.

ABOVE

Blickling's most remarkable interior, the Long Gallery, with its original, heavily symbolic, ceiling by Edward Stanyon and bizarre Victorian frieze by John Hungerford Pollen. The Long Gallery became a library in the 18th century.

that thanks to his aunt, the new Lord Buckinghamshire was in the forefront
of advanced architectural taste, with its new-found enthusiasm for what Lady
Suffolk's friend and neighbour Horace Walpole of Strawberry Hill called
'King James's Gothic'.

The entrance front.

In one of the earliest instances of 'Jacobean Revival', the 2nd Earl of
Buckinghamshire bucked the Classical style and made a series of sympathetic
alterations to Blickling. 'Gothick it was', he told his Aunt Henrietta, 'and
Gothick it will be in spite of all the remonstrances of modern improvers and
lovers of Grecian architecture.'

The Ivory dynasty of architects and craftsmen was brought in from
Norwich to rebuild the west front and part of the north front, and to refash-
ion Lyminge's dramatic staircase with its delightfully dotty series of newel
figures, most of which had to be replaced. The new west front was not
very successful, but the north front is much more in keeping. Even the
texture and bond of the brickwork is hard to distinguish from the genuine Jacobean article.

Not all Lord Buckinghamshire's tickling of Blickling, however, is in
the Jacobean manner – and the great house is none the worse for that.
The old Jacobean withdrawing chamber was partitioned and exotically decorated in the Chinese taste in the early 1760s. Later, in the 1770s, Lord

Buckinghamshire created Blickling's two major 18th-century rooms – the Peter the Great Room and its adjoining state bedroom – in order to commemorate the high point of his career, when he was sent by King George III to be Ambassador in St Petersburg. Portraits of the King and his Queen, Charlotte, together with the rich canopy of state adorn the state bedroom, which may have been completed by Samuel Wyatt after Thomas Ivory had his leg crushed by a piece of timber.

Although endowed with looks and charm, the 2nd Earl does not seem to have deceived his contemporaries as to more sterling qualities. Horace Walpole likened him to a confection known as 'the Clearcake' which was 'fat, fair, sweet, and seen through in a moment'. He was a martyr to gout and, according to Walpole, his death in 1793 was brought about by thrusting his inflamed foot into a bucket of icy water.

Blickling was inherited by the 2nd Earl's younger daughter, Lady Suffield. During her long tenure of Blickling she commissioned Joseph Bonomi to build a pyramidal mausoleum in the park and John Adey Repton to carry out various improvements, all in sympathy with the Jacobean flavour of the house. It was Repton who was largely responsible for the reconstruction of the central clock tower in the 1820s and for the linking arcades between the main house and the wings.

On Lady Suffield's death, childless, in 1850, Blickling passed to her great-nephew, the 8th Marquess of Lothian, who renovated the house with the help of the architect Benjamin Woodward and the decorative painter John Hungerford Pollen, a collaborator of William Morris and Sir Edward Burne-Jones. With the increased appreciation of Victorian taste it can now only be a matter for regret that the 11th Marquess of Lothian should have swept away so much of Pollen's fascinating decoration – which was certainly of more interest than the conventional 'safe' taste that replaced it.

By the time that James Lees-Milne, first secretary of the National Trust's Country House Scheme, saw Blickling during the Second World War it was 'a sad, lonely, unloved house with a reproachful air'. He soon grew to love it, however, for the more he gazed 'the more I was impressed by the dowagerial majesty of this ancient pile; and then bewitched by its rosy brick complexion'. Lees-Milne's diaries and his book *People and Places* paint an evocative picture of the National Trust's sensitive restoration of Blickling. Although, like so many other Trust properties, it is no longer actually a family home (one might say that only an idealistic bachelor such as the 11th Marquess of Lothian could have imagined such a conflicting state of affairs ever being a working reality), Blickling is an outstanding example of a great house beautifully preserved for posterity by expert and sympathetic hands, thanks to the foresight of its former owner.

WOBURN ABBEY

BEDFORDSHIRE

IT IS a curious irony that though Woburn has been a household name since its phenomenal success in the stately home industry of the 1950s, the name itself is invariably mispronounced. Although the old Cistercian abbey in Bedfordshire, granted to the Russell family after the Dissolution of the Monasteries, had always been pronounced 'Wooburn', the 13th (and present) Duke of Bedford, who opened the place to the public in 1955, democratically took to calling it 'Woeburn', so as not to confuse his paying customers.

'Ian' Bedford had inherited the traditional Russell shyness and endured a strange upbringing – he was kept in ignorance of his ducal destiny and was reduced to eating the chocolates put out for his eccentric father 'Spinach' Tavistock's beloved parrots – but he forced himself to face the glare of publicity as a pioneer of 'stately' showmanship. He did so in order to save Woburn Abbey, which would otherwise have had to be sold, owing to the exceptionally heavy death duties incurred by the demise of both his reclusive grandfather and his quixotic pacifist father within a few years.

By the time he inherited the Dukedom in 1953 Woburn and its 16,000-acre estate had fallen into an almost derelict state. In the ensuing years the 13th Duke stopped at virtually nothing so that the great treasure house could be preserved for posterity. The visitors flocked to Woburn and the more discerning found plenty to admire beside the tripperish attractions. Indeed the contents of the house are overwhelming in their variety and splendour: an outstanding collection of 16th- and early 17th-century portraits, including the celebrated 'Armada' portrait of Queen Elizabeth I; later portraits by Van Dyck, Reynolds and John Hoppner; pictures by Frans Hals, Rembrandt, Tintoretto, Murillo, Claude, Poussin and Teniers; and a series of Canaletto views of Venice. The furniture includes marquetry

PRECEDING PAGES
The Palladian west front
of Woburn Abbey glows
in a stormy autumn dusk.

LEFT
View through the
enfilade of state
apartments at Woburn
– a distance of some
220 feet.

RIGHT
Looking down the
cantilevered Great
Staircase, probably built
by Henry Flitcroft for the
4th Duke of Bedford.

commodes by Pierre Langlois, 'Chinese Chippendale', French marquetry
and Boulle; there is fine English and Sèvres porcelain and fabulous services of silver, silver-gilt and gold plate.

Ian Bedford once described the Russells as thinking themselves 'slightly
grander than God'. Certainly they rank with the Cecils of Burghley as
one of the great British families who rose to prominence in the Tudor
age. Originally medieval wine merchants, the Russells had risen to the
status of county gentry in Dorset by the end of the 14th century. The durable
Tudor diplomatist Sir John Russell was given a Barony by King Henry VIII
and created Earl of Bedford by King Edward VI.

LEFT
Dining Room, with screens of Corinthian columns.

RIGHT
Classical stance. The 5th Duke of Bedford suffered a rupture playing cricket; it was later aggravated by a tennis ball, with fatal consequences.

Although the 1st Earl came into possession of Woburn Abbey in 1547, it was not until the early 1600s and the tenure of the 4th Earl of Bedford, who increased the family fortunes by draining the Fens and developing Covent Garden in London, that Woburn came into its own. This Lord Bedford pulled down most of the old monastic buildings and erected a handsome new Carolean house on the same site, perpetuating the courtyard plan.

The interior features included a saloon known as the 'Star Chamber', from the golden astral decorations on its walls, and, most notably, a Fountain Room or Grotto in the north wing. This deliciously cool cavern of shells and stucco is very much in the Italian Mannerist style and, inevitably,

The delightful 17th-century Grotto, originally designed as an open loggia where
the Russell family could sit and breathe in the good clean air of Bedfordshire.
The stonework is carved to resemble seaweed and adorned with shells.

there is a tradition that it must have been designed by Inigo Jones, who was certainly associated with the 4th Earl of Bedford's Covent Garden improvements. The likelihood, though, is that it was designed by Jones's assistant, Isaac de Caus, who also worked at Wilton (see pages 76–85).

The Puritan 5th Earl lived to a great age, and was predeceased by his heir, Lord Russell, who came to be regarded as a martyr to the Whig cause, having been executed after the Rye House Plot of 1683. Eleven years later the Puritan Earl was raised to the Dukedom of Bedford, partly in honour of the memory of his son, who was described in the preamble to the patent of creation as 'the ornament of his age, whose great merit it was not enough to transmit by history to posterity'.

Something Lord Russell was able to transmit to posterity was a vast fortune, enhanced by his marriage to the former Lady Rachel Wriothesley, heiress of the Bloomsbury estate in London. The Russells were at the forefront of the Whig oligarchy, and in the mid-18th century the 4th Duke of Bedford commissioned the architect Henry Flitcroft to give Woburn a Palladian face-lift.

Flitcroft built the long west front, facing the park, with its Ionic centrepiece linked to the wings by two lower ranges. Inside, he created a grand series of state rooms, beginning with the exotic Chinese Room and proceeding through the State Apartment, the State Bedroom, the central Saloon, the State Dining Room and the Breakfast Room to the Carolean Long Gallery, which Flitcroft remodelled. Yet Woburn still lacked a set of family rooms.

These were installed by the bachelor 5th Duke of Bedford, an agriculturalist who brought in the fashionable Whig architect Henry Holland. From 1787 onwards Holland rebuilt the southern range of Woburn Abbey, transforming some old offices into an *enfilade* of handsome living rooms, including a superb Long Library with two pairs of Corinthian columns, and a corner 'eating room', which was hung with Canalettos brought down from Bedford House when the family's London residence was demolished in 1800. Holland was also responsible for creating the enchanting Chinese Dairy, a conservatory, tennis court and riding school.

The 6th Duke of Bedford carried on improvements with the help of Sir Jeffry Wyatville. A keen botanist, the 6th Duke erected flower houses for his plant collections, though he converted Holland's conservatory into a sculpture gallery, and also brought in Humphry Repton to landscape the park. Later in the 19th century Woburn enjoyed a halcyon period when the 7th Duke of Bedford entertained on a princely scale, but subsequently a series of withdrawn, misanthropic Dukes presided in lonely grandeur over feudal formality. The wife of the 11th Duke (who

saved from extinction the Père David deer from China in the park)
took refuge in aviation, becoming famous as 'the Flying Duchess'
before being lost on a solo flight over the North Sea (a room at Woburn
now celebrates her exploits).

In the late 1940s the Flying Duchess's son, 'Spinach', the 12th
Duke, demolished the dry rot-ridden east range by Holland, as well as
the same architect's riding school and tennis court. The neo-Georgian architect Sir Albert Richardson was employed to undertake a tidying-up operation,
which involved flank walls to seal off the truncated wings, and steps leading
up the hill towards Flitcroft's twin mid-18th-century stable blocks.

After 20 bustling years of resuscitating the estate, Spinach's son, the
13th Duke of Bedford, made over Woburn to his eldest son and heir, the
Marquess of Tavistock, who together with his energetic wife, the former
Henrietta Tiarks, has valiantly carried on the constant struggle to make

ABOVE
The results of Sir Albert
Richardson's tidying-up
operation, which set off
Flitcroft's twin mid-
18th-century stable
blocks.

Woburn a paying proposition. Besides opening more rooms – the tour of the house covers three floors, including the crypt – the Tavistocks' enterprises have included pop concerts, an antiques centre, two championship golf courses, a flourishing stud, a pottery, corporate hospitality and catering. In 1985 they gave some Père David deer to the People's Republic of China, where the species has become successfully re-established in its original and natural habitat.

In short, Woburn is a hive of activity and, as Lady Tavistock observed in a television documentary series about the place, the best way to describe the châtelaine's day is 'like running up a down escalator'. The Tavistocks are determined to follow the example of the 13th Duke who, in the words of his son, 'realized the importance of providing a full and enjoyable day out for every member of the family, while preserving the beauty of the house and its setting'.

TREDEGAR HOUSE

GWENT

ALTHOUGH this book is entitled 'Great Houses of England *and* Wales', the Principality is modestly represented for the simple reason that Wales has very few 'great houses'. What it lacks in quantity, however, is amply compensated for in terms of quality by the magnificence of Powis Castle (see pages 30–39), and the curiously little-known Tredegar House in what used to be Monmouthshire and is now called Gwent.

Tredegar is an exceptionally splendid example in brick and stone of that glorious late 17th-century period in architecture when symmetry and the Classical Renaissance still had a slightly rustic, home-bred feel. No architect is known for sure to have worked at this family seat of the Morgans and there are no obvious parallels with other houses. The only possible comparisons that come to mind are with Ragley Hall in Warwickshire and Maiden Bradley in Wiltshire. It happens that the master-carpenters Roger and William Hurlbutt, or Hulbert, from Warwick, worked at both these places and this has led the architectural historian Sir Howard Colvin to suggest that the design of Tredegar might be attributed to either of them.

Overall, the style of Tredegar's principal facade has a 'Dutch' feel, with the brick adorned by carved stone swags round the windows. Inside, one is quite bowled over by the exuberant wood carvings of the Brown Room and the Great Staircase, with its balustrades of scrolling acanthus. The *pièce de résistance* is the gorgeously ornate Gilt Room, with its richly twisted columns and elaborate painted ceiling, illustrating how Pope Urban VII nobly overcame lust.

No precise dates can be put on Tredegar's lavish rebuilding but *circa* 1664 to *circa* 1672, with the fitting-up of the interiors going on well into the 1680s, seems a reasonable presumption. In the course of this 17th-century remodelling the north-east wing of the original medieval house was completely rebuilt, and the old screen wall replaced by an additional wing which was designed as the principal facade. The 17th-century roof was higher than it is today and surmounted by a cupola and balustrade – removed around the end of the 18th and the beginning of the 19th century.

The Morgan family's connection with Tredegar goes back to at least the early 15th century. Sir John ap Morgan was a faithful ally of the ambitious Welshman Henry Tudor, who became King Henry VII, and was rewarded with the post of Constable of Newport Castle. Sir John appears to have rebuilt the house at Tredegar; the surviving south-west wing, which now houses the servants' hall, probably dates from his time.

The most likely person to have carried out the 17th-century remodelling is William Morgan, who married the heiress of another William Morgan, a rich lawyer who was King's Attorney for South Wales. Early in the 18th

PRECEDING PAGES
Tredegar House, from across the lake.

BELOW
The decorative climax of the state rooms at Tredegar, the Gilt Room, with its pine panelling painted to resemble walnut, and gorgeous gilding.

ABOVE
The elaborately carved
doorway of the Brown
Room. A bust of the
Emperor Augustus is
supported by intricately
carved trophies of arms.

century yet another Sir William Morgan of Tredegar married Lady Rachel
Cavendish, daughter of the 2nd Duke of Devonshire of Chatsworth (see
pages 140–49). Judging by the copious Tredegar accounts for coaches, cock-
pits, racehorses, blackamoors, musicians and fancy clothing, this brilliant
match seems to have gone literally to Sir William's head – among other extrav-
agances he found it necessary to procure the services of a French peruke-
(or wig-) maker.

Eventually, in 1792, Tredegar was inherited by Jane Gould, whose
husband, Sir Charles Gould, Bt, Judge Advocate-General and president

LEFT
The Great Staircase:
a 17th-century carved
curiosity, with balustrades
of scrolling acanthus
which may have been
remodelled in the
19th century.

of the world's first life assurance society, the Equitable Life, duly took the name of Morgan. A remarkable tycoon, he successfully exploited the coal and iron on the Tredegar estate and built a chain of canals and tramroads in the neighbourhood.

Sir Charles's son and namesake was probably responsible for the early 19th-century remodelling of the house, to accommodate his eight children and ever expanding household. The surviving warren of servants' rooms at Tredegar bear eloquent witness to the elaborate rituals of 'downstairs' life. In 1859 the next Sir Charles Morgan, the 3rd Bt, was raised to the peerage by Benjamin Disraeli as Lord Tredegar. His son Godfrey took part in the Charge of the Light Brigade and survived into the 20th century to become a generous public benefactor in South Wales. He was advanced in the peerage from a Barony to a Viscountcy.

The 2nd Viscount Tredegar, like many early 20th-century aristocrats, devoted himself largely to hunting, shooting and fishing, but his son, the 3rd Viscount, had more exotic tastes. Indeed this Lord Tredegar, otherwise the artist, poet and novelist Evan Morgan, can claim a niche in the gallery of aristocratic eccentrics. An aesthete with a passion for animals, he maintained a bizarre menagerie at Tredegar which included such creatures as bears, gorillas and kangaroos, with whom His Lordship liked to box. There is a celebrated 1930s photograph of Evan swanning around at one of his numerous garden parties at Tredegar with his parrot, Blue Boy, perched on his shoulder, while the worthy local gentry look on aghast. One of his party tricks, apparently, was to let Blue Boy crawl up his trouser legs and then peep his beak out from the fly buttons.

Evan's luxurious 'Cow Bathroom' (so called because it housed his collection of Staffordshire pottery cows), complete with bidet, evokes Tredegar's 'Indian Summer' as a country house in the 1930s. As it turned out, Evan, who died in 1949, was the last Morgan to live in the house. In the 1950s, Tredegar was sold, and the place became a boarding school run by the Sisters of St Joseph.

By the 1960s Tredegar House had virtually disappeared off the map. Soon afterwards the school was absorbed into the comprehensive system: blackboards, desks and strip lighting dominated the interiors, now painted in institutional colours. It looked as if this great house had gone forever. However, in 1974 Newport Borough Council stepped in and acquired the house, stables, home farm, gardens and 90 acres of parkland. Notwithstanding Tredegar's unpromising position, engulfed by the M4 motorway and the urban sprawl of Newport – and its poor state of repair, aggravated by dry rot and the attention of woodworms – the council determined to restore the building and to present it as a furnished country house.

Thanks to the sympathetic skills of its imaginative curators, who have included David Freeman, Michael Hunter and now Laura Beresford, Tredegar House somehow manages to avoid the deadly atmosphere of a museum. Gradually, some of the original contents are returning – through loan or acquisition. The fascinating old kitchens – featured in the BBC's *Victorian Kitchen* series – have been restocked with antique items, gathered together by the vigorously enthusiastic 'Friends of Tredegar'. This hitherto neglected great house, so surprisingly exhumed, deserves many more friends to discover its unusually atmospheric charms.

ABOVE
The Great Kitchen, with its roasting range, spit mechanism and copper boiler.

RIGHT
One of the atmospheric, evocative corridors at Tredegar.

The entrance front of Tredegar.

CHATSWORTH

DERBYSHIRE

CHATSWORTH, a treasure-trove in the most beautiful of English settings, exemplifies the *beau idéal* of a benevolent, paternalistic ducal estate. In describing many great houses one is tempted to use the past tense for their days of glory are so often long gone; at Chatsworth, though, there is a strong feeling that 'the House' is enjoying its golden age today, under the consummate leadership of the present Duke and Duchess of Devonshire.

In the past the Dukes of Devonshire possessed so many great houses, including the mighty Hardwick Hall nearby (see pages 102–111), that they could only spend part of the year in each, but the present Duke has concentrated his attention on 'the Palace of the Peak'. The result is that Chatsworth has really come into its own for the first time in its long history.

After the Second World War, when Chatsworth became a girls' school, it seemed that the Cavendishes would never live in the house again. Confiscatory capital taxation of '80 per cent of everything' on the death of the 10th Duke of Devonshire threatened to destroy this part of the 'heritage' as it had so many other great houses. During the 1950s numerous landed proprietors retreated to lesser houses on their estates but the present Duke and Duchess decided to give it a go and finally moved back in 1959; today the house is owned by a charitable trust.

The sympathetic and thoroughly practical changes wrought by the present Duchess have redefined life in the country house. A Mitford who writes as well, if not better, than her celebrated sisters, Deborah Devonshire has produced several books celebrating the house, the gardens, the estate, the treasures and her beloved farm animals in an irresistibly breezy way. They capture the *joie de vivre* which permeates the atmosphere of Chatsworth and can be savoured by even the most casual visitor.

Important as the history of the architecture, art and landscape are at Chatsworth, it is the human qualities of a living community that seem to matter more in the scheme of things. The Devonshires and their estate seem psychologically sure of their identity and purpose. Chatsworth succeeds in being at once a working, well-run estate, a tourist attraction, a great house and a family home. The Duke and Duchess do not live in a poky wing: they maintain an unostentatious but fitting ducal style in the most attractive part of the main house and their frank enjoyment of their good fortune is refreshingly infectious. The redecoration and re-ordering of their own apartments – from re-gilding the glazing bars of the windows to adding modern works of art by Lucian Freud and Angela Conner – has shown that the 'heritage' need not be an ossified, museumified affair but a constantly evolving organism. Outside, too, the gardens have been rejuvenated with sculptures by Elisabeth Frink and Angela Conner and imaginative new horticultural designs – such as the Duchess's jolly 'cottage garden'.

The Duke of Devonshire is not being affected when he says that the visitors are 'very welcome'. 'They really are', he adds. 'I would feel uneasy not sharing all this with the public.'

'All this' certainly encompasses a great deal: there are, for instance, 175 rooms, 3,426 feet of passages, 17 staircases, 359 doors and 7,873 panes of glass. Although the original Tudor house cannot be seen, it is there embedded in the skeleton of the central block of the new classical house of the late

PRECEDING PAGES
The 'Palace of the Peak' with its Hunting Tower on the skyline.

LEFT
The Blue Drawing Room which, according to the Bachelor Duke's *Handbook* (when it was called the Music Room), 'used to be the most joyous and frequented of all the rooms at Chatsworth'. It now very much is again for this is the room, overlooking the south, that the present Duke and Duchess use as a family sitting room. The modern family portraits around the jib door are by Lucian Freud; the one actually on the door is of the present Duchess aged 34, though she once heard a visitor observe 'That's the Dowager Duchess. It was taken the year she died'.

ABOVE
The sumptuous library, originally the 1st Duke's Long Gallery, took on its present appearance *circa* 1830. The recently restored ceiling of gilded stucco by Edward Goudge, with paintings by Verrio, dates back to the 1st Duke's time. The bookcases are by Wyatville, the sofas and chairs came from Devonshire House in London, and the portrait of Henry VIII is after the original by Holbein.

The Violin Door in the State Music Room – a brilliant piece of *trompe-l'oeil* which really does deceive the eye. Even close up, it is almost irresistible not to touch it to see if it is real. It was painted by Jan van der Vaart (1653–1727) on a door brought to Chatsworth in the 1830s from the family's London residence, Devonshire House in Piccadilly (demolished in 1924).

The Duke of Devonshire, a devoted bibliophile, takes a nap in the Lower Library. The *Handbook to Chatsworth and Hardwick* (1844) records how John Crace transformed the old breakfast room into 'something between an illuminated manuscript and a café in the Rue de Richelieu... two bearded artists in blouses were imported from Paris and completed the ceilings and pilasters'.

17th and early 18th century. Building operations began at Chatsworth in 1552, five years after the formidable 'Bess of Hardwick' married, as her second husband, Sir William Cavendish, a Suffolk squire who had done well out of the Dissolution of the Monasteries.

By the 1680s the Tudor Chatsworth was found to be 'decaying and weake' so the 4th Earl of Devonshire (created Duke of Devonshire in 1694 for his part in bringing William of Orange to the English throne) set about some improvements. Initially, he only intended to remodel the south front, but he found building so enjoyable that he carried on right the way round, adding a new east front and then the west, finally completing the north front before he died in 1707.

William Talman was the architect for the south and east fronts and Thomas Archer may have been responsible for the west and north, though the Duke himself probably took a hand. Outside, the Duke laid out spec-

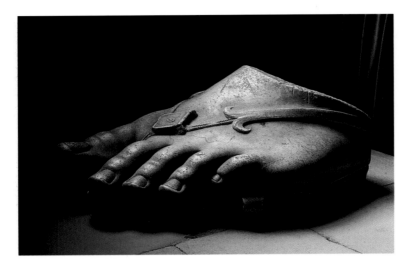

LEFT
A colossal female foot, 1st century BC, in the West Sub-Corridor. It was sold to the Bachelor Duke by the sculptor Carlo Finelli and was formerly in the Quirigi family's palace at Lucca.

tacular water gardens including the Cascade and a 314-yard-long canal. These formal gardens were largely swept away by the 4th Duke in the 1760s at the hands of the ubiquitous Lancelot 'Capability' Brown. The 4th Duke, who married the heiress of the architect 3rd Earl of Burlington, also brought in James Paine to build the monumental stables (now a restaurant) and the bridge over the river which affords such a fine view of the west front.

RIGHT
The bronze figure of Mercury, cast for the Bachelor Duke after the original in Florence by Giambologna, on the Great Staircase. The 1st Duke had the grisaille panels on the wall painted to resemble sculpture. The real sculpture above is by Caius Gabriel Cibber (1630–1700).

The 5th Duke of Devonshire, an idle fellow, married the legendary beauty Lady Georgiana Spencer, immortalized as 'The Face Without a Frown' by Gainsborough and Reynolds. Their son, the 'Bachelor Duke' devoted himself to improving his multifarious properties, particularly Chatsworth. 'I enjoy being here before all earthly things', he wrote. 'I adore it'; and 'I am drunk with Chatsworth.'

The Bachelor Duke's essential *Handbook to Chatsworth and Hardwick* (1844) shines through with his love of the place and his enthusiasm for all he did there. He engaged the architect Sir Jeffry Wyatville to build the long and rather ponderous north wing, which houses many of Chatsworth's state apartments. In the gardens the Bachelor Duke forged a famous partnership with his tubby head gardener Joseph (eventually Sir Joseph) Paxton, a relationship described by the Bachelor Duke's biographer James Lees-Milne as 'one of the most satisfactory in the history of master and man'. They went on expeditions to collect plants and are largely responsible for the present layout of the Chatsworth gardens.

In her own book on *The House* (1982), which brings the 6th Duke's *Handbook* up to date, the present Duchess points out that the Bachelor's

influence on Chatsworth was immense. His benign qualities of generosity and humour apply equally to the present Duchess herself, whose love of jokes and fun illuminates Chatsworth. 'It is a terrible place to house-train a puppy', she observes in *The House*. It is typical of the Duchess to nominate Beatrix Potter as her favourite artist in preference to, say, Veronese, Murillo, Rembrandt and Poussin – all well represented on the walls of Chatsworth.

Perhaps the enchanted world created so meticulously by Beatrix Potter is the key to appreciating the *genius loci* of Chatsworth at the end of the 20th century. The doors of the farm shop, for example, open straight into the pages of *The Tale of Ginger and Pickles* and the award-winning farmyard for children is also pure Potter. For all its grandeur, its frescoed and treasure-filled state apartments, its Old Master paintings, boulle furniture and 17th-century Delft pottery, the peculiar charm of Chatsworth is the way the Duchess, in the words of her friend Elizabeth Winn, 'has managed to turn the whole place into a smallholding'.

The Sculpture Gallery, housing the Bachelor Duke's collection of mythologies, including works by Canova (for example the *Sleeping Endymion with his Dog* in the right foreground). The *Wounded Achilles* (left foreground) is by Filippo Albacini.

PETWORTH HOUSE

SUSSEX

ALTHOUGH Petworth House, the Sussex seat of the Wyndham family, can boast masterpieces by Van Dyck and Titian, as well as a notable series of 17th- and 18th-century Dutch, Italian and French paintings, for once in a great house, the 'home side' comes out on top. Besides fielding such artists and sculptors as Grinling Gibbons, Gainsborough, Reynolds, George Romney, Richard Wilson, John Flaxman and Sir Richard Westmacott, Petworth has two outstanding home-grown stars: 'Capability' Brown and J.M.W. Turner.

The incomparable 18th-century parkland created by Brown inspired Turner in the early 19th century to such an extent that the artist took up residence at Petworth, under the hospitable roof of his friend and patron, the 3rd Earl of Egremont. Turner was given a room to work in, and one of his delightful series of watercolours shows him painting there. A curmudgeonly Cockney, the son of a barber, Turner kept the door locked. No-one was allowed in except Lord Egremont, and he always knocked first.

The results of Turner's labours now adorn the walls of Petworth, and the Tate Gallery in London. A set of watercolour and gouache sketches of the interiors *circa* 1827 has recently inspired the National Trust (which was given the house in 1947 by the 3rd Lord Leconfield) to carry out an ambitious redecoration scheme to revive the spirit of the place during the time of the 3rd Earl of Egremont. As for the exterior, Turner's great oils show a scene which is happily – despite the ravages of the hurricane of October 1987, which destroyed 600 trees in the park – little changed today. In his hauntingly evocative painting of *A Stag Drinking*, Turner depicts Petworth Park at sunset. Clumps of trees throw long shadows across the lake, and in the foreground, in a golden haze, a stag slakes his thirst.

Turner used to say that if he could have begun life again he would rather have been an architect. It is intriguing to speculate what he might have done to Petworth. The present pile, a magnificent baroque palace, was built between 1688 and 1696 by the 'Proud Duke' of Somerset to replace an old manor house, of which little now remains except for the 13th-century chapel. The Proud Duke had acquired Petworth through his marriage to Elizabeth Percy, heiress to Alnwick (see pages 12–21), Syon (see pages 50–57) and the other Percy estates, and widow of the murdered 'Tom o' Ten Thousand' Thynne of Longleat (see pages 94–101). The Percy family had come into the manor in the 12th century and a licence to crenellate was granted in 1309. The 9th 'Wizard Earl' of Northumberland began assembling the fine library at Petworth in the late 16th century, and the 10th Earl started

PRECEDING PAGES
Petworth: the back view of the house across the trees.

BELOW
Looking down from the North Gallery.

collecting the house's great treasury of pictures. The Proud Duke seems to have been under the impression that he was *le Roi Soleil* rather than a Sussex squire, and indeed there is a strong whiff of Versailles about the vast west front – some 320 feet long – at Petworth. The French influence relates it stylistically to the north front of Boughton in Northamptonshire (see pages 150–159), built by the Proud Duke's stepfather-in-law, Ralph Montagu. The architect of the remodelled Petworth is not known. Candidates from the home side who have been floated by architectural historians over the years include John Scarborough, a surveyor, and William Talman, but the French runners, Pierre Puget (a sculptor), Daniel Marot and the

mysterious 'Monsieur Boujet' appear more convincing authors
– particularly Marot, who is known to have worked for Ralph
Montagu and who features, tantalizingly briefly, in the Proud
Duke's personal account book at Petworth.

As a composition, the west front suffers from the lack of
its original squared dome in the centre which, as a picture
of *circa* 1700 shows, relieved the length of the facade. This
dome survived a disastrous fire of 1714, which wrecked much
of the interior of the centre of the house, save for the Marble Hall (a room reminiscent of Het Loo at Apeldoorn in
Holland, where Marot also worked), but was removed at a
later, unknown, date.

Although the identity of the architect is unrecorded, the
various craftsmen are well documented, notably the carvers
John Selden and Grinling Gibbons. Selden's and Gibbons's
best work for the Proud Duke was later installed in the Carved
Room by his great-grandson, the 3rd Earl of Egremont. Horace
Walpole considered Gibbons's luscious pendants and pair
of double picture frames as 'the most superb monument of
his skill', and Selden's efforts are by no means overshadowed.

Upon the death in 1750 of the Proud Duke's son, the
7th Duke of Somerset, the great Percy inheritance was divided.
Alnwick passed to the 7th Duke's daughter, Elizabeth, who
married Sir Hugh Smithson, later the 1st Duke of Northumberland, whereas Petworth, and the Cumberland estates, went
to the 7th Duke's nephew, Sir Charles Wyndham, who also
inherited the Earldom of Egremont. Sir Charles – or the 2nd
Earl of Egremont, as he became – was a notable connoisseur.
To house his statuary the 2nd Earl commissioned Matthew
Brettingham (the Elder) to build him a sculpture gallery,
known as the 'North Gallery' at Petworth; in style it is similar to the same architect's sculpture gallery for Lord Egremont's
friend the 1st Earl of Leicester at Holkham (see pages 194–203).

The hospitable 3rd Earl of Egremont presided over a
halcyon period at Petworth which stretched from almost

RIGHT
The White Library.

ABOVE
Entrance Hall, with
flagged floor.

the beginning of the reign of King George III to that of Queen Victoria. As
well as Turner, the 3rd Earl was the patron of the painters Thomas Phillips
and James Northcote, and the sculptor John Edward Carew. In the 1770s
he hired Matthew Brettingham the Younger to modify the west front at
Petworth, whereby the ground-floor windows were lengthened and the roof
balustraded. Later, the 3rd Earl began extending his father's sculpture gallery,
created the Carved Room and divided the Proud Duke's rectangular dining room into the Square Dining Room and the Somerset Room.

   The 3rd Earl's eldest bastard son was created Lord Leconfield. In 1869
the 2nd Lord Leconfield, concerned about the porous nature of the walls
rebuilt after the fire, invited the architect Anthony Salvin to Petworth for
his advice. 'My Lord', observed this Victorian practitioner after surveying
the spectacle, 'there is only one thing to be done. Pull the whole house down
and rebuild it.' Lord Leconfield replied: 'You'd better see the inside first.'

   In the event, Salvin only rebuilt the south-east part of the house, adding
the new entrance and *porte-cochère*. Another of the 2nd Lord Leconfield's

RIGHT
The Grand Staircase,
decorated with murals by
Louis Laguerre for the
Duke of Somerset after
the fire of 1714 had
destroyed the old
staircase. The balustrade
is by Sir Charles Barry,
circa 1827.

LEFT
A small but impressive
picture gallery surrounds
this chimneypiece in the
Little Dining Room.

building enterprises was a special greenhouse to grow his own bananas. Once he had discovered, however, that the Petworth fruit tasted 'just like any other damn banana!' as he exclaimed, the greenhouse was promptly destroyed.

This and other amusing anecdotes about the family are related in *Wyndham and Children First* by his grandson, John Wyndham, who revived the title of Lord Egremont when he was created a peer on the recommendation of Harold Macmillan, to whom he was private secretary. John's uncle, the 3rd Lord Leconfield, had given the house to the National Trust. Recently the Trust has stylishly recreated the warmth and characterful clutter of the 3rd Earl's time. In doing so, the Trust's experts have the full support and consideration of the present Lord Egremont, who has lent more than 100 paintings for the 're-hang' from his private collection. Max Egremont, who still lives with his wife and family in a wing of the main house, is a distinguished biographer and an original and witty novelist.

RIGHT
The upper reaches at
Petworth.

BOUGHTON HOUSE

NORTHAMPTONSHIRE

IF THE French influence is easily discernible at Petworth (see pages 150–59), it is positively overwhelming at Boughton House in Northamptonshire, where Ralph Montagu, later 1st Duke of Montagu, gave the north front the appearance of a French château. Montagu had developed a taste for French architecture and decoration while serving as British Ambassador to King Louis XIV in Paris from 1669 to 1678, and on his return to England set about giving both his London house in Bloomsbury and his country seat near Kettering a touch of Versailles.

As at Petworth, it is not known for sure who was responsible for the designs adopted, but Daniel Marot seems the most likely candidate to have been the mastermind both at Montagu House (the site of the future British Museum) and Boughton. A Huguenot, Marot fled from France to Holland after the Revocation of the Edict of Nantes in 1685, and soon afterwards became architect to William of Orange, who was shortly to become King William III of England. Ralph Montagu, who had a chequered political career, was a close friend of the Dutch monarch.

A significant element of Boughton's potent charm is how, paradoxically, the place combines French and English features. Beneath the elegant French mask of the north facade lies a characteristically English structure of almost village-like proportions. An aerial view shows 7 courtyards, 12 entrances and 52 chimney stacks; there are also the traditional 365 windows. This agglomeration is explained by the fact that, like so many great English houses, Boughton began life as a monastery. In 1528 Edward Montagu, a lawyer, acquired the property from St Edmundsbury Abbey and tacked on a manor house to the old Great Hall. As Sir Edward rose in power so Boughton grew; courtyards and wings were added in the course of his near-40-year tenure.

PRECEDING PAGES
Boughton: the English
'village' behind the
French facade.

LEFT
The simple panelling,
even in the back
corridors, is one of
Boughton's special
charms.

RIGHT
The Great Hall: the
central feature of the
house. Louis Chéron's
painted barrel ceiling of
the marriage of Hercules
and Hebe was added
circa 1680, obscuring
the ancient hammer-
beam roof structure. The
panelling of Boughton
oak was installed in
1912, when Jan Wyck's
portrait of the Duke of
Monmouth was brought
down from Scotland and
installed above the
fireplace.

Subsequent generations of Montagus continued to add courts and
wings to the hotchpotch of the ancient manor of Boughton. Then, in the
late 17th century, Ralph, the 3rd Lord Montagu of Boughton, decided
to make a bigger splash. The gossipy chronicler Spring Macky, while noting
that Ralph was 'inclining to fat, of a coarse, dark complexion', conceded that
he was 'a good Judge of Architecture and Painting as his fine Pictures at his
Houses in Northamptonshire do show. He hath one of the best Estates
in England, which he knows very well how to improve.' Macky also recorded
that Ralph Montagu was 'a great Supporter of the French, and other Protestants who are drove into England by the Tyranny of their Princes'.

Indeed Boughton is a treasure house of French arts and crafts. The
use of mansard roofing was quite new to England, as was the *parquet
de Versailles* flooring in many of the rooms. The *trompe-l'oeil* walls and
ceilings in the staircase hall are by Louis Chéron, and some of the most

outstanding pieces of French furniture were given to Montagu by *le Roi Soleil* himself, Louis XIV. In the Little Hall there are flower studies by Jean-Baptiste Monnoyer, one of many Huguenot craftsmen brought to England by Ralph Montagu.

    The stables were also given the Versailles treatment and in the park Ralph commissioned a formal layout, involving lakes and canals, from a Dutchman, Van der Meulen. In 1695, some eight years after Ralph began

ABOVE
The late Duchess of Buccleuch's barrel-ceilinged boudoir.

the transformation, Boughton was in a fit state for King William III to be entertained there in splendid style.

Ralph was made Earl of Montagu by King William III in 1695, and advanced to a Dukedom by Queen Anne ten years later – 'a distinction', *The Complete Peerage* insists, 'beyond his merits'. His son John, the 2nd Duke of Montagu, Master General of the Ordnance, was more interested in planting trees than building. He failed to finish his father's great scheme at Boughton – hence 'the Unfinished Wing' – but planted avenues of trees which at one time totalled 70 miles in length. Subsequently Boughton was inherited by John's granddaughter, Elizabeth, who had married the 3rd Duke of Buccleuch.

The Buccleuchs descend from the ill-fated Duke of Monmouth, to whom Ralph Montagu had given his support (and consequently spent five years in exile in France) when, in 1685, Monmouth challenged his uncle James II's right to the throne. Monmouth was King Charles II's bastard son by his first mistress, Lucy Walters. Monmouth himself had married the heiress of the Scotts of Buccleuch, and besides the family seats of Bowhill in the Vale of Ettrick and Dalkeith near Edinburgh, the 3rd Duke of Buccleuch also inherited the spectacular Baroque castle of Drumlanrig in Dumfriesshire from his Douglas cousin, the 4th Duke of Queensberry, in addition to his wife's property of Boughton.

RIGHT
A vertiginous view down the back staircase.

It was therefore inevitable that Boughton drifted away from the centre of the stage in the lives of the Montagu Douglas Scotts, as they became called, one of the greatest territorial dynasties in Europe, who owned some 460,000 acres in the 19th century. Boughton House, largely untouched since 1700, fell into a state of slumber. Fortunately, as so often happens, its apparent neglect proved a blessing in disguise. The late-Georgian, Victorian and Edwardian 'improvers' passed it by, serving only to enhance its almost tangible air of timelessness.

A century and more passed. Then, in the 1920s, the bride of the heir to the Dukedom of Buccleuch, Mollie Lascelles, a spirited young lady with consummate taste, fell in love with the sleeping beauty of Boughton. She determined to bring it back to life.

She succeeded triumphantly, harmoniously blending the superb collections of paintings, furniture, tapestries, carpets, porcelain, arms and silver in a series of simple yet grand panelled rooms. She made Boughton much

LEFT
Entrance doorway at the end of a colonnade.

more than a showcase, however, and ranks with Sybil Cholmondeley at Houghton (see pages 184–93) as one of the great châtelaines of the 20th century. Mollie Buccleuch's *cavaliere servante*, the writer Alan Pryce-Jones, described her as 'visibly descended from the Lady Bessborough who cut a swathe through London Society two centuries ago; she would have been perfectly at home in the Devonshire House of 1820'.

At Boughton, as Pryce-Jones relates in his memoirs, the Duchess entertained 'not only Ambassadors and Royal Duchesses, but off-beat writers... museum experts; dogged American millionaires, who required a nap after luncheon, [and] soon tired of Raphael cartoons, Carlin writing tables and Isfahan carpets'. One of the 'off-beat writers', the aesthete Brian Howard (part model for the character of 'Anthony Blanche' in Evelyn Waugh's *Brideshead Revisited*) drooled: 'I have never been in such a magical place, so full of beautiful things.'

Mollie Buccleuch, widowed in 1973, stayed on at Boughton until her death in 1993. Today, while remaining the home of the present Duke and his family, the house is a focal point for Sotheby's study courses – appropriately enough, in view of its visually unrivalled collections of armour, tapestries, Old Masters, portraits, English and French furniture, Sèvres porcelain, to name but a few – and the estate, in the form of the Living Landscape Trust, is an award-winning pioneer in improving schoolchildren's understanding of the countryside. In 1997 Boughton became the first historic house to have its own website on the Internet.

What strikes the visitor to Boughton is the gracious understatement of the architecture and the panelled interiors. Here is a beguiling lesson in the difference between late 17th-century taste and the more flamboyant ostentation that came soon afterwards.

CASTLE HOWARD

YORKSHIRE

THE APPROACH to Castle Howard, Yorkshire, through the Howardian Hills, is probably the most dramatic of all the great houses of England and Wales. The five miles of avenue stretch up and then down before you, punctuated by a series of architectural fanfares – the huge monument to the 7th Earl of Carlisle; the exotic Carrmirre Gate by Nicholas Hawksmoor with its pyramids; the mock-fortified curtain walls and gatehouse by John Vanbrugh; and then the 100-foot Obelisk, marking the intersection of avenue and drive.

The Obelisk has an inscription recording how 'Charles the III Earl of Carlisle of the Family of the Howards Erected a Castle where the Old Castle of Henderskelfe Stood and Call'd It Castle-Howard. He Likewise Made the Plantations in this Park and All the Other Out-works, Monuments and Other Plantations Belonging to the Same Seat'. The 'Old Castle of Henderskelfe' had only been rebuilt in 1683 but ten years later was gutted by fire. The ambitious young Lord Carlisle, who rose to be First Lord of the Treasury, was determined to build a palatial new pile befitting his grand status. In 1698 he commissioned William Talman, the architect who had worked at Chatsworth (see pages 140–49), to draw up some Classical designs but the two promptly fell out. The next year Lord Carlisle took the surprising step of entrusting the design of Castle Howard to someone who had never designed a building before, the playwright John Vanbrugh, an acquaintance at the Kit-Cat Club, a haunt of Whig grandees where 'Van's' wit and style were much appreciated.

Although brimful of imagination and confidence Vanbrugh had little idea of how to put his grandiose ideas on to paper, but in the spring of 1699, the same year as he was approached by Lord Carlisle, he met the

perfect collaborator in Nicholas Hawksmoor, the best-trained professional architect of his day, who had studied under Wren. Hawksmoor became
Vanbrugh's right-hand man and they worked in tandem at Castle Howard
and later at Blenheim (see pages 176–183).

Together with Lord Carlisle they set about transforming an unpromising chunk of the North Riding of Yorkshire – 'bushes, bogs and briars' as
Vanbrugh put it – into a Classical arcadia. The most notable of the many
original touches in the design of the main house was a central dome; no private house had had a dome before, though those at St Paul's Cathedral and
the Royal Hospital at Greenwich (in which Hawksmoor had a hand)
were currently much in the news.

For all his grandeur Lord Carlisle did not have unlimited funds and
building work on Castle Howard, which began in earnest in 1700, proceeded at a sedate pace. By 1714, when the Obelisk was erected, the
centre block with its dome, the south front, the east wing and the Kitchen
Court were more or less complete, but nothing had been done about the
west wing. Ten years later Vanbrugh, becoming understandably impa-
tient, was pleading that the loose stones near the site of the west wing should
be used for its foundations.

PRECEDING PAGES
A wintry view of the
garden front from the
south-east. Vanbrugh broke
all the rules – setting the
house on a north/south
axis and inserting a dome
in the middle of his
composition – but carried
it off with theatrical style.

RIGHT
A corner of 'Brideshead'.

BELOW
The Long Gallery, one of
the interiors designed by
Tatham, 1801–11. The
Norwegian oak bookcases
were installed in 1827. The
1725 table on the right has
a Peterhead granite top.

By this stage, though, Lord Carlisle was more concerned about his 'Out-works'. Vanbrugh's last design at Castle Howard, before his death in 1726, was the Temple of the Four Winds at the end of the grass terrace – another domed affair but on a miniature scale with four Ionic porticoes and carved finials. This exquisite building and Hawksmoor's noble domed Mausoleum, beyond the bridge over the New River, are the highlights of any visit to Castle Howard. Even Horace Walpole was to wax lyrical: 'Nobody had informed me at one view I should see a palace, a town, a fortified city, temples on high places, woods worthy of being each a metropolis of the Druids, the noblest lawn in the world fenced by half the horizon, and

LEFT
A glimpse of the Great Hall, 'a dramatic slice of Baroque Cathedral inserted into an English house'. The dome, destroyed in the fire of 1940, was restored in the 1960s by George Howard, later Lord Howard of Henderskelfe.

Flower arranging in the Great Hall, in front of Bacchus's Niche – one of the earliest examples in England of the use of scagliola, a mixture of hard plaster and marble chips.

a mausoleum that would tempt one to be buried alive; in short, I have seen gigantic palaces before, but never a sublime one'.

Unfortunately, Lord Carlisle's son-in-law, Sir Thomas Robinson, fancied himself as an architect and badgered his brother-in-law, the 4th Earl of Carlisle, to let him complete Castle Howard. It was Robinson who was responsible for the long – in fact, too long – west wing, finally built between 1753 and 1759. While perfectly handsome, this Palladian exercise does not chime sympathetically with the *sprezzatura* style of Vanbrugh. 'Long Sir Tom' also had the satisfaction of destroying the two rooms at the end of the south front.

Fortunately, before he could do further damage to Vanbrugh's legacy, Robinson's enterprises were curtailed by the death of his brother-in-law and the succession to the Earldom of Carlisle of ten-year-old Frederick, whose trustees were not inclined to continue building operations. Frederick's main contribution to Castle Howard, apart from collecting the Italian paintings for the Orleans Room, was commissioning C.H. Tatham to finish the interior of the west wing, notably the Long Gallery, the Museum Room and the Chapel.

LEFT
View up to the dome in
the Mausoleum – a
building that tempted
Horace Walpole to be
buried alive.

The 9th Earl of Carlisle was a talented painter in the Pre-Raphaelite manner and a friend of Sir Edward Burne-Jones, whose designs for the stained-glass windows in the chapel were executed by William Morris. This Lord Carlisle tidied up some of Robinson's less happy efforts on the west wing but largely left the running of the place to his formidable wife, 'Radical Rosalind', who came from the high-minded dynasty of Stanley of Alderley, a staunch teetotaller and an alarmingly illiberal Liberal.

Rosalind rode roughshod – to be more precise, she advocated barefootedness – over the principles of primogeniture and on her death in 1921 bequeathed Castle Howard, according to her feminist principles, to her eldest daughter, Lady Mary Murray. Lady Mary, however, preferred to stay on in Oxford with her husband Professor Gilbert Murray, the Greek scholar, and it passed to a younger brother, Geoffrey Howard.

During the Second World War Castle Howard, like several other great houses (including Chatsworth), was occupied by a girls' school. One night in November 1940 a fire broke out which gutted the east and central sections of the south front and destroyed the dome. Molten lead cascaded from the burning dome to the floor 70 feet below. Several sumptuous interiors, including the High Saloon and Garden Hall, with their Pellegrini murals and mirrored walls, were lost.

Vanbrugh's masterpiece was a forlorn shell, seemingly destined for dereliction. The trustees, assuming that Castle Howard would never be lived in again, had begun to sell the contents when Geoffrey Howard's son, George (later a life peer as Lord Howard of Henderskelfe), returned from the war. An expansive, vigorous figure, he confounded all the Jeremiahs and proceeded to move in.

He and his wife, Lady Cecilia (daughter of the 8th Duke of Grafton), opened the house and park regularly to the public from 1952 and, 20 years after the fire, succeeded in restoring the dome. He commissioned the Canadian artist Scott Medd to re-create Pellegrini's fresco of Phaeton's fall so that once more the climax of the interior, the Great Hall, is an inspirational *tour de force*, resembling, as Mark Girouard has written, 'a dramatic slice of a Baroque Cathedral inserted into an English house'.

Another of George Howard's outstanding re-creations was the new Garden Hall in the spirit of Vanbrugh with the help of the architect Julian Bicknell and the artist Felix Kelly. Kelly's panels depict imaginary, indeed fantastic, follies that might have been designed by old 'Van' himself. It is a charming conceit, a fitting tribute to Vanbrugh's genius and a permanent reminder of Castle Howard's claim to international fame, as the setting – even star – of Granada Television's lavish film of Evelyn Waugh's romantic novel *Brideshead Revisited*. For the Garden Hall is the room in which we saw Jeremy Irons (as Charles Ryder) dabbing away with his paintbrush at the panels on the wall. Like the narrator of the novel, any visitor to Castle Howard can conclude '*Et in Arcadia Ego...*'

RIGHT
Hawksmoor's great
Mausoleum looming
above the hayfields.

BLENHEIM PALACE

OXFORDSHIRE

SURVEYING the ornately Baroque palace in Oxfordshire built in honour of the 1st Duke of Marlborough's smashing victory at Blindheim, or Blenheim, in Bavaria in 1704, King George III muttered that he had 'nothing to equal this'. Indeed there can be little doubt that Blenheim is the greatest palace in Britain, far outstripping those in possession of the Royal Family. Some of its interiors, notably Sir John Vanbrugh's Great Hall and Saloon and Nicholas Hawksmoor's Library, can vie with the most splendid palace rooms in Europe.

Yet for all that, ever since building operations began on the old royal estate of Woodstock, granted by 'a munificent Sovereign', Queen Anne, to the triumphant Marlborough in January 1705, Blenheim has tended to receive somewhat mixed notices from its visitors. Sir Winston Churchill – Blenheim's most famous son, who was born in the palace in 1874 and was actually heir to the Dukedom of Marlborough until the birth of his cousin 'Bert' in 1897 – maintained loyally that 'the cumulative labours of Vanbrugh and "Capability" Brown have succeeded in setting an Italian palace in an English park without apparent incongruity'. Bert's widow, on the other hand, Laura Duchess of Marlborough, described Blenheim in her memoirs as 'so terribly gloomy... built as a monument not a house to live in'. To her it was always known as 'The Dump'.

To complain of Blenheim's lack of homeyness, however, is rather beside the point. The object, after all, was not only to house a national hero but to celebrate England's newly won supremacy over the French in a blaze of architectural glory that would rival Versailles. The triumphal mood of Vanbrugh's dramatic composition is everywhere apparent – from the Grinling Gibbons carvings of English lions lacerating French cocks on

PRECEDING PAGES
The Great Hall: cool, marbled, majestic and 67 feet high. The Duke of Marlborough's banner hangs above the front door.

LEFT
The elaborate 'door furniture', or lock, on the front door of the palace, copied from the gates of Warsaw.

the towers, to the trophies on the entrance steps underneath the giant portico presided over by Pallas Minerva, goddess of victory. On the ceiling of the cool marbled Great Hall within, the 1st Duke of Marlborough, kitted out by the artist Sir James Thornhill as a Roman general, shows the Blenheim battle-plan to Britannia.

Naturally, the state apartments at Blenheim were not intended to be 'lived in'; they were for pomp and parade. Vanbrugh designed the east wing for the family to base themselves and they are there to this day. The central block and the west wing were to comprise courtly chambers in which to entertain the Sovereign. In the chapel, Marlborough, attired in Roman armour, stands atop a monument so noble as to make you wonder whether one is supposed to be worshipping God or the Great Duke.

BELOW
View across the Water
Terraces on the west side
of Blenheim. The terraces,
designed by the 9th Duke
of Marlborough and the
French landscape designer
Achille Duchêne, have
been compared to the
parterre d'eau at
Versailles and constitute
a remarkable 20th-
century achievement.

Born plain John Churchill in Devon in 1650, he became one of the
very few men in British history to rise from obscure beginnings to a dukedom. He owed his early advancement to the fact that his sister Arabella
was a doxy of the Duke of York (later King James II) and, quite possibly, his
own romps with King Charles II's tempestuous mistress, Barbara Villiers.

The building of Blenheim Palace remained a source of delight and diver-
sion to the 1st Duke of Marlborough to the end of his life in 1722, even
if its long drawn-out labours became the despair of his Duchess. Sarah
Marlborough had wanted Sir Christopher Wren as architect, but Queen
Anne, and the Duke himself, opted for John Vanbrugh.

Following his triumph at Castle Howard (see pages 168–75) for the
3rd Earl of Carlisle, 'Van' had become effectively Wren's No.2 at the Board
of Works – a remarkable achievement for an amateur. Marlborough knew

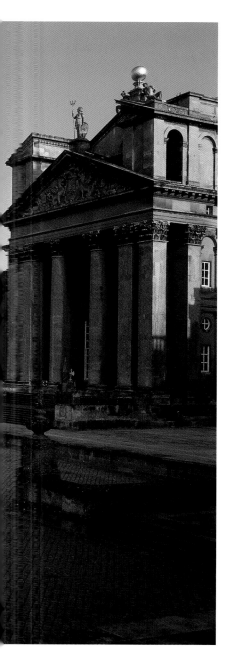

'Van' through their joint membership of the Kit-Cat Club. As the site of the new palace Vanbrugh chose a broad plateau at the southern end of Woodstock Park which appealed to his sense of theatre. In front, to the north, was a dramatically steep valley down to the River Glyme. On the other side of the valley were the picturesque ruins of Old Woodstock Manor.

In his biography of Vanbrugh's right-hand man, Nicholas Hawksmoor, Laurence Whistler points out that 'though Blenheim as a whole is Vanbrugh's, yet there is not one detail of which one could say with certainty that Hawksmoor had not designed it'. Certainly Hawksmoor helped Vanbrugh lay the foundation stone in June 1705 and his hand can be clearly detected in various commissions carried out for Duchess Sarah after the Duke's death. Duchess Sarah had fallen out spectacularly with Vanbrugh, who described her as 'that BBBB old B the Duchess of Marlborough'.

Sarah lived on until 1744, having completed the Gallery, the Chapel and the Column of Victory, which was designed by the amateur-architect 9th Earl of Pembroke, who built the exquisite Palladian bridge at Wilton (see pages 76–85). Yet it was not until the time of the 4th Duke of Marlborough, a scholarly connoisseur who reigned at Blenheim from 1758 to 1817, that the palace really came into its own as a family seat. The 4th Duke brought in Sir William Chambers to carry out various minor improvements about the place and commissioned 'Capability' Brown to landscape the park. Brown's new lakes at Blenheim, giving full point to Vanbrugh's bridge, represent, as Sir Sacheverell Sitwell observed, 'the one great argument of the landscape gardener. There is nothing finer in Europe'. Yet the way he grassed over Vanbrugh's and Henry Wise's superb formal gardens was nothing short of vandalism.

Happily, however, in the 1890s and early part of the 20th century, the 9th Duke of Marlborough, an historically minded if arrogant man, decided to make what amends he could. In the Great Court he restored the formal arrangement and to

LEFT
Looking across the grand entrance to the family's private apartments in the east wing.

the east and west created new formal gardens. The 9th Duke's Water Terraces on the west front are a remarkable modern achievement and undoubtedly one of the finest features of Blenheim. Together with the French landscape designer Achille Duchêne, he set out to construct a sort of *parterre d'eau à la Versailles*. The result was more Italian and Classical in style than French.

Today Blenheim is one of the most popular 'stately homes' on the 'heritage trail', but the present Duke and Duchess of Marlborough still maintain a ducal presence in the east wing, where the Duchess – formerly Countess Rosita Douglas, a Swedish fashion designer – has stylishly redecorated the private apartments. It is noticeable that the present generation of Marlboroughs, unlike many of their predecessors, have a genuine affection for Blenheim, which is, indubitably, far from a 'dump'.

LEFT
Sir Joshua Reynolds's grandiose group of the 4th Duke of Marlborough and his family, which hangs in the Red Drawing Room. The 1st Duke is represented by the statue on the right of the picture. The 4th Duke, who reigned at Blenheim for nearly 60 years is shown in his Garter robes, holding one of his sardonyx collection. His heir, the 5th Duke, grasps a box containing some of the Marlborough Gems.

RIGHT
The Saloon, which was decorated with murals by Louis Laguerre after Sir James Thornhill was sacked by Sarah Duchess of Marlborough (she thought his painting 'not worth half a crown a yard' let alone the 25 shillings he charged). Laguerre (who inserted himself among the figures depicted) charged £500 for the job. The result is one of the most splendid palace rooms in Europe.

HOUGHTON HALL

NORFOLK

THE role of the châtelaine in the modern age has been of vital importance to the rejuvenation of several great houses, as exemplified by the late Countess of Ancaster at Grimsthorpe (see pages 68–75), Lady Victoria Leatham at Burghley (see pages 86–93), the present Duchess of Devonshire at Chatsworth (see pages 140–49), the late Duchess of Buccleuch at Boughton (see pages 160–67) and, by no means least, the late Marchioness of Cholmondeley at Houghton Hall in Norfolk.

When the Earl of Rocksavage, heir to the 4th Marquess of Cholmondeley, married Sybil Sassoon, descendant of banking sheikhs from Baghdad, in 1913, the Palladian palace of Houghton, which had passed to the Cholmondeleys from the Walpole family, was in a bad state. The 3rd Earl of Orford – grandson of the first 'Prime Minister', Sir Robert Walpole, who built the house in the early 18th century – had removed the two sets of grand exterior steps to save the cost of repairs, and sold the fabulous picture collection to the Empress Catherine of Russia to meet his gambling debts in 1779. In the 19th century Houghton was offered for sale to both the Duke of Wellington and the Royal Family.

Fortunately Sybil Cholmondeley (as she became in 1923 when her husband inherited the marquessate), like her brother the politician and socialite Sir Philip Sassoon, Bt, had an eye for beautiful things and she could afford to collect and conserve. An exotic beauty of the Edwardian era – her striking dark features were captured by John Singer Sargent – she retained an aura of old world luxury into the last dozen years of the 20th century.

At Houghton she carried out a superb restoration of the house, made good the gaps in the collections with paintings, French furniture and porcelain of the highest quality and, above all, replaced the double staircase which rises in front of the basement to the *piano nobile* on the west front. The steps bear a Latin inscription which, freely translated, reads: 'These stairs which were built by Robert Walpole and removed by his grandson were rebuilt for Houghton Hall in 1973 to their original design in memory of George 5th Marquess of Cholmondeley'.

The 'original design' to which the inscription refers was drawn up by the Palladian architect Colen Campbell, who prepared the plans for Houghton in 1721. His client, Sir Robert Walpole, had not only recently become Prime Minister and Chancellor of the Exchequer, but had also inherited the family estate of Houghton near King's Lynn on the death of his father.

The Walpoles had held the manor of Houghton since the late 12th century, and were then seated in a Jacobean house. Robert Walpole had begun collecting Old Master paintings before he inherited Houghton, and when his father died in 1720 he determined to create a splendid setting for his pictures. Having studied Campbell's plans he then engaged his protégé, Thomas Ripley, a carpenter who had married one of Walpole's servants, to take charge of the building operations.

Ripley took the sensational step of using Aislaby sandstone, brought by sea from Yorkshire. It proved a master-stroke. For Aislaby stone is extremely durable, and its cool, creamy gold colour has weathered the east wind wonderfully over the centuries.

As the chatty Lord Hervey observed, the 'base or rustic storey' at Houghton was for 'hunters, hospitality, noise, dirt and business', while from the entrance hall (which runs the width of the house), rises the staircase to the *piano nobile*, designed 'for taste, expense, State and parade'. The 'taste and expense' was entrusted to a brilliant team of artists and craftsmen. The sculptor John Michael Rysbrack executed statues of Britannia and Neptune on the east front, and a heroic chimneypiece in the Stone Hall, a 40-foot cube with a stucco ceiling and frieze of *amorini* by the Venetian Giuseppe Artari.

The star of the show, however, is William Kent, who Walpole brought to Houghton in 1727. Houghton is Kent *in excelsis*. His hand is everywhere. He painted the staircase walls in grisaille and designed the Tuscan pedestal for the bronze gladiator by Le Sueur. In the spectacular Saloon, he not only painted the deeply coved ceiling in gold mosaic, but designed everything from the gilt sofas and stools to the pier tables and glasses. The Green Velvet Bedchamber contains one of Kent's most sublime creations, a culmination of all that is exquisite at Houghton – a state bed covered in sumptuous green velvet with architectural needlework and a giant cockleshell in the headboard.

PRECEDING PAGES
The approach to Houghton with a view of the east and north fronts.

RIGHT
Looking from the Stone Hall to the Great Staircase.

Sir Robert Walpole took great delight in the building and decoration of Houghton, which carried on until 1735. Yet in truth he had overspent in his lavish creation of Houghton, and he left his descendants an expensive pile to maintain.

By 1781 Horace Walpole was comparing the decay of Houghton with the loss of the North American colonies. 'You and I', he wrote to his old friend Sir Horace Mann, 'have lived long enough to see Houghton and England emerge, the one from a country gentleman's house to a palace, the other from an island to an empire, and to behold both stripped of their acquisitions and lamentable in their ruins.'

Ten years later Horace himself succeeded to the family Earldom of Orford, but at 74 he was too old to up sticks from his beloved Gothick villa

LEFT
Sir Robert Walpole, the first 'Prime Minister'
and builder of Houghton, by John Wootton.

ABOVE
The Marble Parlour, or dining room, with
Bacchic overmantel relief by Rysbrack,
and another Kent ceiling.

ABOVE
A detail of the exquisite Green Velvet
Bedchamber. Green is the rarest colour in
velvet, yet at Houghton hundreds of yards
must have been used. The design of this
shell-like bower was by Kent.

RIGHT
The climax of the Houghton interior: the
Saloon, a case of *Kentissimo* – William Kent at
his best. The portrait above the splendid
chimneypiece is of Catherine the Great, to whom
the 3rd Earl of Orford sold Sir Robert Walpole's
great collection of pictures. The Empress gave
Lord Orford this portrait in return.

at Strawberry Hill in Middlesex to move to Norfolk. On his death six years later, in 1797, the Earldom (created for Sir Robert Walpole in 1742) became extinct and the Houghton estate was inherited by his great-nephew George, 4th Earl of Cholmondeley from a Cheshire family who had been seated at Cholmondeley since the 12th century.

George married Lady Georgiana Bertie, second daughter of the 3rd Duke of Ancaster and sister of Lady Willoughby de Eresby, châtelaine of Grimsthorpe Castle (see pages 68–75). It was through this marriage that a share of the hereditary office of Lord Great Chamberlain of England came into the Cholmondeley family – they hold this position during alternate reigns.

George, who was advanced to the Marquessate of Cholmondeley, decided to remain in Cheshire and rebuilt Cholmondeley as a Gothick castle, so Houghton became a secondary seat. His successors also continued to base themselves at Cholmondeley Castle throughout the 19th century, but on the marriage of the 4th Marquess's heir, the Earl of Rocksavage, to Sybil Sassoon in 1913, Houghton was handed over as a wedding present, and a new golden age began.

ABOVE
Houghton's east front (reminiscent of the palaces of Vicenzo) and the white deer.

ABOVE
The West front, with its
proud new double
staircase.

In Sybil's memory, her grandson, David, the 7th and present Marquess and Lord Great Chamberlain, has recently replanted the walled garden. Inside, the Stone Hall has been emptied of all but its original furniture of mahogany benches and side-tables and the White Drawing Room now has more of the Regency feel without the 18th-century French furniture. The sheer quality of Houghton makes superlatives redundant: this is a house that can rival anything in Europe.

HOLKHAM HALL

NORFOLK

ONLY a few miles down the road from Houghton (see preceding pages) in north Norfolk is another even grander Palladian palace at Holkham, the seat of the Coke family, Earls of Leicester. The house is on a scale worthy of a continental sovereign prince. Going from one to the other in the same day, as many visitors do, offers as noble a prospect as can be experienced anywhere in the world.

Holkham is a staggeringly vast monument to the Augustan Whig confidence of the 18th century; even its four pavilions (double the usual number) would, on their own, constitute a sizeable country house anywhere else. Comparisons with Houghton are inevitable, but the mood and atmosphere of the two places are surprisingly different, despite the fact that they are both Palladian in concept, and that they both draw on the genius of William Kent.

Whereas Houghton was built of Aislaby stone brought in from outside the county, Holkham was constructed of locally baked yellow-grey brick, which from a distance looks like stone. And whereas Sir Robert Walpole, though an enthusiastic follower of the arts, was essentially an amateur patron who left the details to experts, his friend and neighbour Thomas Coke of Holkham (later the 1st Lord Lovell and 1st Earl of Leicester) was very much a hands-on connoisseur. Indeed, unlike Walpole, he was actually a member of the Earl of Burlington's Palladian group; and had learnt, and collected, much on his six-year-long Grand Tour, during which, in Italy, he met 'the *Signoir*', William Kent (then still studying to be a 'history painter' under the patronage of Burrell Massingberd).

The three of them – Burlington, Kent and Coke – formed a committee of taste to plan Coke's new seat at Holkham in the 1720s. The old family home, an Elizabethan manor house, was demolished as unworthy of this disciple of Andrea Palladio. Undaunted by a site that was little more than a bare windswept heath overlooking the North Sea, Coke was set on recreating the glory that was Rome. He began planting trees to improve the landscape but his ambitious building plans hung fire after he lost much of his fortune in the 'South Sea Bubble' speculation of 1720.

Thereafter the creation of Holkham proceeded at a fairly cautious pace; indeed it was only completed in 1762, three years after the death of Coke, or the Earl of Leicester as he then was. There is no doubt that the

The Marble Hall:
Derbyshire alabaster,
fluted pink Ionic
columns, coved and
coffered ceiling.

final result – when the foundations were at last laid in 1735 – was the responsibility of Coke himself (by now Lord Lovell), who had definite ideas of how he wished the house to look. The original designs were pared down to achieve a greater purity, even austerity.

The most stupendous interior at Holkham is the Marble Hall, which rises from basement level up through the *piano nobile*, surrounded by no less than 18 fluted Ionic columns, to a richly coffered and ornamental ceiling. The impression is of a vibrant combination of pink, ivory, purple and green, emanating from the Derbyshire alabaster used lavishly for the columns and lower walls. The agriculturalist Arthur Young memorably observed that it all resembled a great bath waiting to be filled.

Up the stairs one comes to a magnificently proportioned progression of state rooms leading to the Statue Gallery, an enlarged version of Lord Burlington's gallery at Chiswick House. The walls are lined with niches for the antique busts Coke picked up on his Grand Tour, and the gilded furniture, covered in velvet, is by Kent.

Along the garden front we find an *enfilade* of splendid rooms, the Saloon in the centre, all hung with crimson Genoese velvet and major pictures, and with gilded ceilings and doorcases. The fine works of art at Holkham include paintings by Claude and Poussin, Rubens's *Holy Family*, portraits by Van Dyck, and tapestries from Brussels and Mortlake.

That the visitor to Holkham can enjoy such a dazzling Coke's tour owes as much to the builder's wife, Lady Clifford in her own right. It was she who always kept the building accounts and she pressed on with the completion of Holkham after her husband's death in 1759. Her nephew by marriage and successor, Thomas Coke, was to reign at Holkham for some 65 years and made the estate famous through his agricultural improvements.

A pioneer of the Agricultural Revolution 'Coke of Norfolk' shocked his fellow landowners by farming some of his ever-expanding acreage directly himself. Like the sensible fellow he was, Coke of Norfolk (who eventually consented to being created Earl of Leicester) made few changes to the big house at Holkham, which obviously did not need any. He did, however, commission the sculptor Sir Francis Chantrey to execute a series of busts and reliefs on Whig themes in the Marble Hall. To put matters into the proper Norfolk perspective, the sculptor also carved a plaque depicting the two woodcocks he himself killed with one shot while staying at Holkham in November 1829.

RIGHT
The curving colonnade of the Marble Hall gallery.

BELOW
The Green State Bedroom, the principal bedroom at Holkham Hall, where Princess Victoria (later Queen) slept in 1835. The picture above the fireplace is Hamilton's *Jupiter Caressing Juno*; the tapestries are from Brussels and Mortlake; the furniture by Kent.

LEFT
'Coke of Norfolk' in distinctly non-agricultural mode: a reminder of his dashing youth in Rome by Pompeo Batoni. The picture was commissioned by Coke's lover, Princess Louise of Stolberg (wife of Bonnie Prince Charlie), and her features can be detected on the statue of the Vatican Ariadne in the background.

As well as being sculpted by Chantrey, Coke was portrayed in earlier days by Thomas Gainsborough (perhaps the artist's last portrait). We see him in appropriately rustic mode, loading his gun, with a dead bird and frisky dogs at his feet. Another study of the even younger Coke, however, by Pompeo Batoni, reveals an unsuspected side to the great agricultural reformer. In this picture, painted in Rome during young Thomas's Grand Tour, there poses a surprisingly effete young gentleman, togged up in fancy dress and carrying a feathered hat.

Coke of Norfolk died in 1842 and the Holkham tenantry erected a column crowned by a wheatsheaf in his memory, to the designs of W.J. Donthorne. This structure to the north of the house 'answers' the obelisk by William Kent to the south. Coke of Norfolk's son and successor, the 2nd Earl of Leicester, another eminent agriculturalist, added the rather unsightly Victorian *porte cochère* to the entrance front and, even more unhappily, replaced the glazing bars in the windows with plate glass. It is good to record that the present Earl of Leicester, has recently replaced the glazing bars, restoring the exterior of Holkham to its true glory.

There is an endearing photograph showing four generations of the family together at Holkham in 1908: the octogenarian 2nd Earl of Leicester, an endearing old buffer with a woolly beard lying recumbent in a carriage, with the future 3rd, 4th and (a babe in arms) 5th Earls standing respectfully beside the conveyance. Between them, Coke of Norfolk, his son (the 2nd Earl of Leicester) and grandson (the 3rd Earl) reigned at Holkham for an amazing total of 165 years.

The present Lord Leicester is a campaigning president of the Historic Houses Association and a model landlord who has commissioned portraits of his estate staff to hang at Holkham. The house is open regularly to the public and the attractions include a bygones museum, traction engines, a farm centre, a pottery, a deer park and a private beach for visitors. The estate is so vast that Holkham feels like a world apart, and in the centre is the apotheosis of the English Palladian movement.

BELOW
The north front from across the lake on a high summer evening.

HAREWOOD HOUSE

YORKSHIRE

IN the late 1750s Edwin Lascelles of Harewood decided to build a palatial new seat on the Wharfedale estate in the West Riding that his father,
Henry Lascelles, had bought in 1739 with his newly acquired fortune
from the West Indies. Henry Lascelles, who came from a long-established
Yorkshire family, had died in 1753, leaving his son the adjoining estates
of Harewood and Gawthorpe, where he had made his home in the Old Hall.

Edwin wanted a grander seat to match his plutocratic inheritance, and
chose as its site the south-facing hill slope overlooking Gawthorpe Old Hall
and the sweep of countryside beyond. He favoured a Palladian pile with a
portico overlooking the valley, and eventually commissioned the local architect John Carr of York to draw up the plans, after considering the ideas of
Sir William Chambers from London.

While Carr was building stables for the house in 1759, Lascelles showed
the York architect's drawings to Robert Adam, the ambitious young Scot,
fresh from his neo-Classical studies in Italy. Adam proposed various mod-
ifications without disturbing Carr's plans. 'I have thrown in large, semi-circular
back courts with columns betwixt the house and wings', he wrote to his
brother James, also an architect. 'It affords me the greatest pleasure', replied
James Adam, 'that you have tickled it up so as to dazzle the eyes of the squire.'

Lascelles, however, was not the sort of man to be easily dazzled, and
compromised on the design of the exterior between Carr's and Adam's ideas.
The interior, though, was left largely to Adam and the results were indeed
dazzling – all the more admirable in view of the restraints that the gritty
Yorkshire tycoon placed on his designer. 'I would not exceed the limits of
expense that I have always set myself', he admonished Adam. 'Let us do
everything properly and well, *mais pas trop*.'

PRECEDING PAGES
The newly restored,
77-foot-long Gallery at
Harewood, a triumphant
combination of Adam,
Chippendale and
Old Masters. The
mythological paintings
in the ceiling are by
Biagio Rebecca.

LEFT
The garden front from
across the park. The
fence and trees in the
foreground have recently
been removed to give a
better perspective to
the house.

The exterior was finished in local yellow stone in 1765, the decoration by 1772, when 'Capability' Brown submitted plans for enlarging the lake and surrounding it with plantations artfully dotted around on the slopes. Gawthorpe Old Hall was duly demolished and Edwin Lascelles moved into the new house. To make his furniture, Lascelles chose another local man – by then established as an 'upholder' in London – the great Thomas Chippendale from Otley.

The combination of all these glittering talents – Carr of York, Adam, Chippendale and Brown – made Harewood into a great house *par excellence*. Watercolours by Thomas Girtin, Turner and John Varley record something of the original building's delightful charm. Yet, alas, the Arcadian ideal did not appeal to early Victorian taste. In 1843 Sir Charles Barry, architect of the new Houses of Parliament, was commissioned to remodel the house in a rather heavy-handed Italianate style, which involved adding a storey for bedrooms and a massive balustrade, the loss of the portico and the installation of elaborate terraces with fountains.

A detail of the Gallery, as re-organized by Alec Cobbe to show off the best things at Harewood to their greatest advantage. The Chippendale furniture here is probably the finest ever made in England. Besides the exquisite marquetry and gilding, he also made the pelmets, the pier glasses and many of the picture frames.

The terraces and the garden front, showing Barry's heavy balustrade. (Since this photograph was taken, the terrace has been significantly altered, with Barry's planned *parterre* reinstated.)

Barry's clients were the 3rd Earl of Harewood and his redoubtable Countess, formerly Lady Louisa Thynne from Longleat (see pages 94–101). The builder of the house, Edwin Lascelles, was created Lord Harewood in 1790 but as he was childless the Barony died with him and the estate passed to a cousin, Edward Lascelles, who was elevated to an Earldom. When Louisa took up residence in 1841 she found a house virtually unaltered since Edwin's day. She resolved to bring it up to date. Piped water and all manner of modern conveniences were introduced.

The next significant changes at Harewood came about in the time of the 6th Earl, who inherited the fortune of his eccentric great-uncle, the 2nd Marquess of Clanricarde in 1916. He proceeded to put his legacy to magnificent use in buying a superb series of Italian masterpieces, including works of the Florentine Renaissance and from the Venetian school. There are Madonnas by Bellini and Catena, a *St Jerome* by Cima and portraits by Titian, Veronese and Tintoretto. The collection grew to be one of the finest in private hands in England and Wales.

After the First World War, when Harewood had been a convalescent hospital, the house needed extensive renovation and restoration, but the 6th Earl soon had it in fit shape for a princess – for his bride was Princess Mary, later The Princess Royal, only daughter of King George V.

The Princess Royal filled the rejuvenated gardens with new flowering trees and shrubs, and Harewood was entering a halcyon era when the Second World War broke out. The house again became a hospital, and

the family moved into the east wing. The estate provided large amounts of timber and food for the war effort.

Soon after his return from the war the Harewoods' elder son, George, found himself faced with a daunting inheritance. On the death of his father in 1947 the estate had to be reduced from 20,000 to 7,000 acres in order to meet the exorbitant death duties, and shortly afterwards Harewood was obliged to enter the 'stately home industry'. It did so to such good effect that soon upwards of 300,000 visitors a year were arriving to see not only the house and grounds but also such attractions as a bird garden, exhibitions, an award-winning education centre and shops, and to avail themselves of restaurants and adventure playgrounds.

The present Lord Harewood and his second wife, the former Patricia Tuckwell from Australia, share a passionate commitment to the arts, and recently they have carried out a sensational restoration at Harewood which has brought out the house's great qualities to the full. The aim has been to turn the clock back to the golden era of Edwin Lascelles, Adam and Chippendale.

Beginning with the repainting of the Music Room, with its roundels by Angelica Kauffmann, the Harewoods brought in Alec Cobbe, whose phenomenal 'eye' has enlivened so many great houses in modern times to re-hang what had been the Green Drawing Room but is now known as the Cinnamon Drawing Room. Silk for the walls was specially woven in France, the ceiling was cleaned, and the room now contains the work of important English artists such as Reynolds and Gainsborough. The Rose Drawing Room, which has a carpet by Adam, has also received the Cobbe treatment, but the climax of the interior is the Long Gallery.

This great room is now once again everything Adam dreamed of, and a good deal more besides. Adam's chimneypiece, which Barry had shifted to the dining room, surrounded by 19th-century portraits, has been reinstated in the centre of the Gallery's east wall. The main windows opposite are once more adorned by pillars and pilasters.

Yet this is far from being a merely academic 'Adamesque' revival. For the gloriously spacious Gallery – which completely fills one pavilion of the house and almost attains the proportions of a triple cube, 77 feet long – also shows off to amazing advantage two of Harewood's most outstanding features: the Italian masterpieces collected by the 6th Earl and a veritable phalanx of Chippendale mirrors, two of them newly discovered and re-assembled.

The idea of concentrating the great collection of Italian pictures in one place came from Alec Cobbe, who has masterminded the complete renovation of the Gallery. Certainly these walls were designed for pictures, and it makes excellent sense to hang the best ones in the best room under a lofty ceiling featuring mythological paintings by Biagio Rebecca.

As for Chippendale's furniture on display at Harewood, the superlatives are inadequate. Sufficient to say that here the visitor will find probably the finest furniture ever to be made in England – from pelmets and picture frames to marquetry and gilt side tables, rosewood and ormolu, inlaid satinwood and all the rest of it. The Younger Chippendale also chipped in with gilded side tables and 'Egyptian' tables.

Having so successfully answered the conflict of taste between Robert Adam and Sir Charles Barry in the Gallery and elsewhere, Lord Harewood still poses a bold challenge to the visitor in the entrance hall, which is dominated by Jacob Epstein's massive naked *Adam* (from the Garden of Eden, rather than Scotland), carved from a single piece of alabaster. Whether or not this ape-like apparition contributes to Robert Adam's notions of unity or design must be left to the visitor's viewpoint – though the statue itself leaves little to the imagination.

KEDLESTON HALL

DERBYSHIRE

WHEN Doctor Johnson and James Boswell visited Kedleston Hall in
Derbyshire in the autumn of 1777, the sage's biographer was struck by
the magnificence of Robert Adam's building (finished a dozen years earlier for Sir Nathaniel Curzon, 1st Lord Scarsdale), delighted with the extensive
park and filled with 'a sort of respectful admiration' for the number of
old oaks. 'One should think', said Boswell, 'that the proprietor of this must
be happy', to which Dr Johnson replied: 'Nay, Sir, all this excludes but
one evil – poverty.'

In fact, the 1st Lord Scarsdale was not a particularly rich man and
the building of the palatial Kedleston overtaxed his resources. Another contemporary observer, Horace Walpole, remarked that it was 'too expensive
for Lord Scarsdale's estate'. Robert Adam's masterpiece is certainly worthy of a Duke; indeed it was used as the seat of 'the Dukes of Broughton' in
the BBC television series *Nanny*.

The Curzons have owned the Kedleston estate for nearly 900 years,
the proud family motto being 'Let Curzon holde what Curzon helde'. In
the closing years of the 17th century Sir Nathaniel Curzon, 2nd Bt,
whose father had been created a Baronet by King Charles I, pulled down
the old manor house here and replaced it by a red-brick building to the
design of Francis Smith of Warwick. Sir Nathaniel's elder son, John, considered enlarging Kedleston shortly before his death in 1727 to the
designs of James Gibbs, but the 4th Bt did not proceed with the plans. It
was left to the 5th Bt, another Nathaniel, who inherited Kedleston in 1758,
to aggrandize the family seat.

Young Nat, who had been on a somewhat truncated Grand Tour
and collected paintings, wasted no time in putting his ideas into practice.

A fervent admirer of Palladio and of the Earl of Leicester's monumental new pile at Holkham (see pages 194–203), he had Lord Leicester's architect and builder Matthew Brettingham up to Derbyshire within a month of coming into his patrimony. The red-brick house, old stables and outbuildings were swept away, as was the village in front of them.

Brettingham began work on the family pavilion – which remains the residence of the present Lord and Lady Scarsdale to this day – in 1759, but by this time Sir Nat was already having second thoughts about his choice of architect. James Paine arrived on the scene, but Palladian architecture and Rococo decoration were by now being outstripped by neo-Classicism and Sir Nat was enthused by the drawings of Robert Adam.

Initially, though, Adam was only brought in to design the buildings of the park – a ravishing collection including the cascade bridge over the lake, the boathouse and the fishing house. By the spring of 1760, however, the precocious and pushy young Scot had assumed control of the whole building operation.

On the north, or entrance, front, Adam had little option other than to retain the main features designed by Brettingham and Paine, but he managed to make the central portico more dramatic. As the Marble Hall within was to be top-lit, he arranged for the planned windows to be replaced by niches and medallions in the manner of a Greek or Roman temple.

PRECEDING PAGES
Kedleston: the south front, illustrating Robert Adam's ideas of 'movement' in architecture.

RIGHT
The promenade through the Drawing Room, where James Paine's alabaster Venetian window was 'improved' by Adam.

LEFT
Adam's atrium: the Marble Hall, 67 feet by 42 feet and 40 feet high. The floor is of local Hopton Wood stone inlaid with Italian marble; the huge Corinthian columns (25 feet high) are of veined local alabaster. The plasterwork is by Joseph Rose and his team.

BELOW
Detail of an abandoned
mermaid, sporting herself
on a sofa in the Drawing
Room.

RIGHT
The curving 'Family
Corridor', hung with
Curzon portraits.

Although this front has a monumental grandeur, it is the garden, or
south, front that is much more exceptional. This, of course, is entirely Adam's
design. As a central feature he drew on the inspiration of the Arch of
Constantine in Rome, combined with the low, stepped dome of the
Pantheon. This brilliant design gives the south front an uncanny feeling
of what Adam called 'movement'.

Inside, Adam's hand is detectable everywhere, right down to the design
of the inkstands. The celebrated Marble Hall, however, is not as pure Adam
as is popularly believed: the fluting of the alabaster columns was done against
his advice and the stucco ceiling is not one of his own. Beyond the Marble

Hall comes Adam's Saloon, a circular Roman temple with a lofty coffered dome. To the left are the three rooms devoted to music, painting and literature, the paintings inset into the walls as Sir Nat and Adam arranged them; and to the right of the Great Apartment. Of all the rooms at Kedleston, the Dining Room seems the purest Adam. Horace Walpole considered this, 'the Great Parlour', 'in the best taste of all'. The delicacy of Adam's work at Kedleston is a joy to behold. What particularly lifts the spirits is that it seems all of a piece: house, contents, gardens and park combine to form a splendid Georgian ensemble, with the old parish church adding a reassuringly intimate touch.

The central panel on the south front records, in Latin, the completion of the building in 1765 and the dedication of Lord Scarsdale (as he had become in 1761) 'for his friends and himself'. This nicely illustrates Sir Nat's hospitable nature, but his generosity and extravagance in building and furnishing such a great house within barely half a dozen years left his descendants a difficult inheritance to maintain.

ABOVE
Adam's sober and masculine Library, employing the Doric order and geometric patterns.

In the 19th century the successive Lords Scarsdale, notwithstanding their title, their ancient name and their magnificent palace were really 'just ordinary country gentlemen', as their descendant, the great George Nathaniel Curzon, 1st Marquess Curzon of Kedleston, Viceroy of India and Foreign Secretary, put it. Very few alterations were made to the house in that time and the Kedleston of George Nathaniel's childhood had the atmosphere not so much of a palace as of a parsonage, for his father, the 4th Lord Scarsdale, was in Holy Orders.

A pioneering conservationist, the great Lord Curzon restored and redecorated his beloved family seat with exemplary care. He was a founder member and lavish benefactor of the National Trust and it was only appropriate that, in the 1980s, the Trust finally took on Kedleston after a worrying time for the present Viscount Scarsdale when it looked as if this great Georgian ensemble might be dispersed. Eventually, in 1987, an unprecedented grant of £13.5 million from the National Heritage Memorial Fund enabled the majority of the contents of the house to be purchased for the National Trust, and an endowment to be set up for future maintenance. For his part, Lord Scarsdale generously gave the house and park to the Trust, and was able to stay on in the family pavilion with his wife, thus ensuring Kedleston's future and upholding the family motto – 'Let Curzon holde what Curzon helde'.

BELOW
The birds may have flown but the Curzons are still there... looking across the bridge to the north (entrance) front.

BELVOIR CASTLE

LEICESTERSHIRE

THE GOLDEN vision of Camelot, on a wooded hill high above the Vale of Belvoir, that greets the visitor to Belvoir Castle in Leicestershire, seat of the Dukes of Rutland, might strike some as a little too good to be true. Indeed, on closer inspection, the castle turns out to be a Regency construction, yet the towers and bastions are somehow justified by the site's long and romantic history.

Belvoir, otherwise Belvedere, was granted to William the Conqueror's standard-bearer at the Battle of Hastings, one Robert de Todeni. It passed from his descendants, the Albinis, to the family of de Ros when the heiress of Belvoir, Isabel de Albini, married the 1st Lord de Ros in 1246. In Tudor times it was inherited by the Manners family. Thomas Manners, 1st Earl of Rutland, rebuilt the ruinous castle from the 1520s onwards. Later in the 16th century the 5th Earl was implicated in the Earl of Essex's plot against Queen Elizabeth I and was thrown into the Tower of London, but recovered his lands on the accession of King James I, whom he entertained at Belvoir. The castle's vicissitudes continued during the Civil War when it was first held for the King, then besieged and surrendered, and finally demolished by the Cromwellians with the reluctant consent of the 8th Earl of Rutland, who was himself of mildly Parliamentarian sympathies. After the Restoration of King Charles II, Belvoir was rebuilt yet again, this time as a fairly plain house; the stables of the present castle are contemporary with this 17th-century rebuilding.

The 9th Earl of Rutland was to the fore in rallying support for William of Orange and the 'Glorious Revolution'. Celebrated for his hospitality, he sheltered Princess Anne at Belvoir during these troubled times, and as a reward she created him Duke of Rutland when she acceded to the throne.

His grandson, the 3rd Duke of Rutland ('a nobleman of great worth and goodness', according to the not usually charitable Horace Walpole), nurtured a special affection for Belvoir and was known as 'the Old Man of the Hill'. In about 1750 he carried out various improvements to the house, adding the Picture Room with cellars underneath. The Old Man of the Hill's son and heir, the Marquess of Granby, was the most celebrated member of the Manners family. He distinguished himself at the Battle of Minden in 1759 and went on to command the British forces during the remainder of the Seven Years' War. Popular with his troops, he is commemorated by numerous public houses up and down the country, the signs bearing his benevolent bald-headed features.

It was not until the dawn of the 19th century that a new and fitting Belvoir Castle finally took shape. The 5th Duke and his Duchess, the former Lady Elizabeth Howard from Castle Howard (see pages 168–75), wanted

PRECEDING PAGES
Belvoir Castle: Regency Camelot.

BELOW
The Guard Room: Belvoir's overwhelming Gothic entrance hall, adorned with arms and armour.

RIGHT
The Grand Staircase,
rebuilt by the Gothic
enthusiast Sir John
Thoroton after the
fire of 1816.

a fairy-tale structure and promptly commissioned one from James Wyatt, who had by then switched from the neo-Classical to the Gothic style and was engrossed in building William Beckford's fantastic and ill-fated Fonthill Abbey in Wiltshire. The Belvoir project was hardly less ambitious and almost as ill-starred.

Although progress was slow, by the time Wyatt died in 1813, two of the new fronts were finished, the crested and turreted chapel contrasting with a mammoth neo-Norman tower. In the same year the Prince Regent came to Belvoir and was presented with the key to the castle.

Three years later, in October 1816, disaster struck. A terrible fire roared through the new castle early one morning, wrecking most of Wyatt's work. The north-east and north-west fronts were completely destroyed. The worst losses, though, as the 5th Duke of Rutland wrote sadly to the Prince Regent, were the pictures collected by his father. About half the collection, including works by Reynolds, Titian and Van Dyck, perished in the blaze.

The romantic vision of the 5th Duke and his Duchess, however, was not extinguished by the flames and they turned to the Duke's chaplain, the Reverend Sir John Thoroton, to pick up the pieces. A Gothic scholar, he did his best, but he was hardly an adequate substitute for James Wyatt. To help him, he had the services of Wyatt's sons, Benjamin, Philip and Matthew Cotes Wyatt.

Buttressed by the Rutlands' coal fortune and with the enthusiastic and knowledgeable support of Duchess Elizabeth, the new team plugged gamely on until the enormous castle was finished about ten years later. Whatever its shortcomings, the final result was, as the diarist Charles Greville noted, 'so grand as to sink criticism in admiration'.

Sadly Duchess Elizabeth died in 1825, aged 45, and never saw the fully completed article. Her presence lives on, though, in the lavish Elizabeth Saloon in Thoroton's eastern tower. Her life-size statue in marble by M.C. Wyatt dominates the room, which has a ceiling depicting the amours of Jupiter and Juno, luxurious Louis XV white and gold panelling and furniture upholstered in rose-red damask silk.

The 7th Duke of Rutland (better known as the romantic Tory politician, Lord John Manners, the friend of Disraeli, who portrayed Belvoir as 'Beaumanoir' in his novel *Coningsby*), succeeded to the castle in 1888 and delighted in maintaining what the old gossip Augustus Hare delighted to call 'mediaeval ways' at Belvoir. Trumpeters would parade the passages sounding the time to dress for dinner and watchmen would call the hours through the night – which must have made it hard to enjoy a good sleep. The 7th Duke's granddaughter, the venerable beauty Lady Diana Cooper, who lived on into the 1980s, recalled in her autobiography how her grandfather would wrap himself in a thick black cape when walking along the chill corridors of Belvoir. She also recorded how much the 7th Duke enjoyed opening Belvoir to the public, and the 'look of pleasure and welcome on his delicate old face' as he watched the populace pouring in.

The 11th and present Duke of Rutland continues to open Belvoir regularly to the public. The attractions include medieval jousting tournaments

LEFT
The Chapel, with the Manners family gallery above the altar. The picture over the altar is Murillo's *Holy Family*; above the family gallery hangs Gaspard Poussin's *Last Supper*. The recumbent marble figure (bottom left) is the nine-year-old Lord Haddon, sculpted from a model by his mother, Violet Duchess of Rutland; a copy is at Haddon (see pages 22–9).

and the regimental museum of the 17th/21st Lancers (the 'Death or Glory Boys'). Thoroton's headily Gothic Guard Room has a high vaulted ceiling, vistas through a complex arrangement of arches and displays of weapons associated with the Leicestershire Militia. Despite the bad losses in the fire of 1816 much remains to be seen in the Picture Gallery, including works by Poussin, Gainsborough and the younger van de Velde.

Belvoir is particularly popular as a location for films – *Little Lord Fauntleroy*, starring Sir Alec Guinness, was one of the many productions filmed there – and its air of romance has an irresistible appeal that has entranced artists from Turner onwards.

WADDESDON MANOR

BUCKINGHAMSHIRE

WITH Waddesdon Manor in Buckinghamshire, completed barely a century ago and now being superbly restored, it is possible to end this chronicle of great houses with a very big bang. For this sumptuous treasure house of the Rothschilds, designed in the French Renaissance taste, is on the grandest scale, and the quality of craftsmanship and connoisseurship is nothing short of staggering.

All around the large estate and the great house itself the eye is caught by a distinctive symbol, five arrows bound in a sheaf. This heraldic device signifies the five sons of Mayer Amschel Rothschild (1744–1812), founder of the celebrated Frankfurt banking house, financial adviser to the Elector of Hesse-Cassel and patriarch of the Rothschild dynasty. His eldest son succeeded his father at Frankfurt, and the four younger sons were sent out, like arrows, to found banking houses in London, Paris, Vienna and Naples.

Baron Ferdinand de Rothschild, a grandson of the founder of the family's Austrian branch, settled in England in the 1860s and married his English cousin, Evelina, younger daughter of Baron Lionel de Rothschild, the first Jewish MP, who was seated at Tring Park in Hertfordshire. One day, out hunting, Baron Ferdinand spotted a bare hilltop outside Aylesbury which he thought might have possibilities. Although by now, in the 1870s, a widower, Baron Ferdinand was set on staying in England and keen to acquire an estate of his own.

He discovered that the Waddesdon estate belonged to the 7th Duke of Marlborough, of Blenheim (see pages 176–83), and duly acquired the property of some 2,700 acres. If his Buckinghamshire neighbours were surprised by such an unlikely purchase, they were astounded when the bare hillside suddenly acquired many hundreds of fully grown trees.

Sometimes 16 horses were needed to haul up the larger trees. Similarly, after the hill had been levelled and planted, Bath stone and other building materials were brought halfway up the hill by a specially constructed steam tramway, and then hauled to the top by teams of Percheron mares, imported from Normandy.

It was not only the horses that came from across the Channel, but the architect, the landscape gardener, the architectural style and most of the contents too. As soon as Baron Ferdinand had signed the contract with the Duke of Marlborough he set out for Paris 'in quest of an architect'. He settled on Gabriel-Hippolyte Destailleur.

In Baron Ferdinand's view, the French 16th-century style was particularly suitable to the surroundings of the site he had selected. He felt it was 'more uncommon than the Tudor, Jacobean or Adam of which the country affords so many and such unique specimens'.

The interior of Waddesdon was lavishly fitted up in the French 18th-century taste. Most of the panelling Baron Ferdinand had installed came from historic Parisian houses destroyed in the traffic-widening schemes of the 1860s. This was no fancy 'repro' but the genuine article.

These elegant rooms were the perfect setting for the Baron's marvellous collections of Savonnerie carpets, furniture by Jean-Henri Riesener, Sèvres porcelain and *objets d'art*. One of the most remarkable items of furniture Baron Ferdinand acquired was P.A. Caron de Beaumarchais's cylinder-top desk, adorned with *trompe l'oeil* documents.

PRECEDING PAGES
Waddesdon roofscape.

RIGHT
A corner of the Baron's Room, showing the cylinder-top desk of 1779 traditionally given by his friends to P.A. Caron de Beaumarchais, author of *The Marriage of Figaro* and *The Barber of Seville*, and music-master to the King of France's daughters. This masculine treasury is adorned with portraits of actresses and singers.

BELOW
A corner of the Chilterns that is forever France.

Yet not everything is French at Waddesdon. There are collections of Chinese vases, Meissen porcelain, Dutch paintings, two enormous canvases of Venice by Francesco Guardi and a splendid set of English portraits by Reynolds, Gainsborough, Romney and Lawrence. Indeed one of the joys of Waddesdon is the way Baron Ferdinand, with his sure, perfectionist's eye, confidently mingled French pictures and furniture with 18th-century English portraits.

In the opulent Red Drawing Room, for example, Gainsborough's portrait of Lady Sheffield in a blue dress is set off by the neighbouring Savonnerie carpet and Riesener commodes. In his own very masculine sitting room (the

ABOVE
A corner of the Grey Drawing Room. The six-fold tapestry screen was made at the Savonnerie factory near Paris after 18th-century designs by Desportes, which were much used at the French court.

RIGHT
The Red Drawing Room, with its gilt armchairs covered in mid-18th century Beauvais tapestry and a chest of drawers made by Jean-Henri Riesener for Louis XVI's sister, Madame Elisabeth, in 1778.

'Baron's Room') Baron Ferdinand surrounded himself with beguiling portraits of beautiful actresses and singers.

Baron Ferdinand, who was in residence in the main part of the house by 1883, entertained on a princely scale. The guests ranged from writers Guy de Maupassant and Henry James to the Prince of Wales, who in 1889 palmed off the erratic Shah of Persia on the long-suffering 'Ferdy'. The next year Queen Victoria herself came out of her customary seclusion to inspect this exotic corner of France in Buckinghamshire. Her Majesty, Baron Ferdinand noted, 'partook of every dish, and twice of cold beef' at luncheon and 'took away three copies of the bill of fare'.

In 1898 Waddesdon passed to Baron Ferdinand's sister, Alice, a formidable but kindly châtelaine who added to the works of art and improved the estate. On Alice's death in 1922 Waddesdon was inherited by her great-nephew, James de Rothschild, a politician and racehorse owner. His wife, Dorothy ('Dollie') Pinto, shared her husband's commitment to Zionism and to Waddesdon. Although Dollie shunned publicity, she was a tireless worker for charitable causes and wrote a delightful book, *The Rothschilds at Waddesdon* Manor (1979), about the beloved house which she and 'Jimmy' did so much to preserve.

During the Second World War Waddesdon became a residential nursery for young London evacuees from the Blitz. On Jimmy's death in 1957 he bequeathed the house to the National Trust, but Dollie stayed on as châtelaine. She died in 1988, aged 93, and since then her heir, the present Lord Rothschild, has masterminded a magnificent restoration programme to show the great Waddesdon treasures to their best advantage.

The idea is not only to bring the presentation up to museum standards but to make the house live, in the same way as Jacob Rothschild has achieved the triumphant restoration of Spencer House in London. Many more rooms are to be opened to the public once the restoration is complete, and the most sophisticated forms of scholarly conservation and lighting are being deployed. In 1999 a suite of three prints and drawings rooms were opened high up in the west tower with spectacular views over the Aylesbury Vale. They contain some 1,600 drawings of the decorative arts from the collection of Baron Edmond de Rothschild, Jimmy's father.

In the grounds, too, the aviary has been restored; the parterre, with its Giuliano Mozani fountain of Pluto and Proserpine, from the ducal palace of Colorno, has been faithfully replanted in the original bright colours by Beth Rothschild (Jacob Rothschild's second daughter); and the old dairy complex, complete with picturesque lake and rock garden, imaginatively re-created by Julian Bannerman.

Baron Ferdinand feared that Waddesdon would 'fall into decay' but hoped that 'the day yet be distant when weeds will spread over the garden, the terraces crumble into dust, the pictures and cabinets cross the Channel or the Atlantic, and the melancholy cry of the night-jar sound from the deserted towers'. A century on, his nightmares have not been realized, and Waddesdon – thanks to the National Trust and above all to the taste, imagination and munificence of Jacob Rothschild – has become a fantasy of substance that can be shared by everyone.

ABOVE

The Grey Drawing Room is dominated by two splendid portraits by Joshua Reynolds: on the right is Lady Jane Halliday and on the left Mrs Abington as the Comic Muse.

ADDRESSES AND CONTACT DETAILS

ALL the 25 houses featured in this book are open regularly to the public. Full details of the facilities, opening times, price of admission, etc., can be found in the annual directory, *Hudson's Historic Houses and Gardens* (published by Norman Hudson & Co, Upper Wardington, Banbury, Oxfordshire). Below are given the addresses, Ordnance Survey map references and telephone numbers of the 25 houses (in alphabetical sequence) featured in this book for ease of reference. Callers from outside the UK should add 44 and omit the first 0.

ALNWICK CASTLE,
Alnwick, Northumberland
NE66 1NQ
OS NU187 135
Tel: 01665-510777

BELVOIR CASTLE,
nr Grantham, Lincolnshire
NG32 1PD
OS SK820 337
Tel: 01476 870262

BLENHEIM PALACE,
Woodstock, Oxfordshire
OX20 1PX
OS SP441 161
Tel: 01993 811091

BLICKLING HALL,
nr Norwich, Norfolk
NR11 6NF
OS TG178 286
Tel: 01263 738030

BOUGHTON HOUSE,
nr Kettering,
Northamptonshire
NN14 1BJ
OS SP900 815
Tel: 01536 515731

BURGHLEY HOUSE,
Stamford, Lincolnshire
PE9 3JY
OS TFO48 062
Tel: 01780 752451

CASTLE HOWARD,
nr York, North Yorkshire
YO60 7DA
OS SE716 701
Tel: 01653 648444

CHATSWORTH,
nr Bakewell, Derbyshire
DE45 1PP
OS SK260 703
Tel: 01246 582204

GRIMSTHORPE
CASTLE, nr Bourne,
Lincolnshire PE10 0NB
OS TF040 230
Tel: 01778 591205

HADDON HALL,
nr Bakewell, Derbyshire
DE45 1LA
OS SK234 663
Tel: 01629 812855

HARDWICK HALL,
Doe Lea, nr Chesterfield,
Derbyshire S44 5QJ
OS SK463 638
Tel: 01246 850430

HAREWOOD HOUSE,
nr Leeds, West Yorkshire
LS17 9LQ
OS SE311 446
Tel: 0113 288 6331

HOLKHAM HALL,
nr Wells-next-the-Sea,
Norfolk NR23 1AB
OS TF885 428
Tel: 01328 710227

HOUGHTON HALL,
nr King's Lynn, Norfolk
PE31 6UE
OS TF792 287
Tel: 01485 528569

KEDLESTON HALL,
nr Derby, Derbyshire
DE22 5JH
OS SK312 403
Tel: 01332 842191

KNOLE, Sevenoaks,
Kent TN15 0RP
OS TQ532 543
Tel: 01732 462100

LONGLEAT HOUSE,
nr Warminster, Wiltshire
BA12 7NN OS ST809 430
Tel: 01985 844400

PENSHURST PLACE,
nr Tonbridge, Kent
TN11 8DG
OS TQ527 438
Tel: 01892 870307

PETWORTH HOUSE,
Petworth, West Sussex
GU28 0AE
OS SU976 218
Tel: 01798 342207

POWIS CASTLE,
nr Welshpool, Powys,
SY21 8RF
North Wales
OS SJ195 001
Tel: 01938 554338

SYON HOUSE,
Brentford, Middlesex
TW8 8JF
OS TQ173 767
Tel: 020 8560 0883

TREDEGAR HOUSE,
Newport, Gwent
NP2 9YW, South Wales
OS ST290 852
Tel: 01633 815880

WADDESDON MANOR,
nr Aylesbury,
Buckinghamshire
HP18 0JH
OS SP740 169
Tel: 01296 651211

WILTON HOUSE,
nr Salisbury, Wiltshire
SP2 0BJ
OS SU099 311
Tel: 01722 746720

WOBURN ABBEY,
Woburn, Bedfordshire
MK43 0TP
OS SP965 325
Tel: 01525 290666

SELECT BIBLIOGRAPHY

BATEMAN, John, *The Great Landowners of Great Britain and Ireland*, London, 1883 (4th edn)

BEARD, Geoffrey, *The Work of Robert Adam*, Edinburgh, 1978

BEDFORD, John, Duke of, *A Silver-Plated Spoon*, London, 1959

BENCE-JONES, Mark, *Ancestral Houses*, London, 1984

—— *The Catholic Families*, London, 1992

BENCE-JONES, Mark, and MONTGOMERY-MASSINGBERD, Hugh, *The British Aristocracy*, London, 1979

BRUYN ANDREWS, C. (ed.), *The Torrington Diaries*, London, 1934–8 (4 vols)

BURKE, Sir Bernard, *Burke's Peerage, Baronetage and Knightage*, London, 1826–1999 (106 editions)

—— *Burke's Landed Gentry*, London, 1833–1972 (18 editions)

—— *A Visitation of the Seats and Arms of the Noblemen and Gentlemen of Great Britain and Ireland*, London, 1852–5 (4 vols)

—— *Burke's Dormant and Extinct Peerages*, London, 1969 (reprint)

BURNETT, David, *Longleat*, 1978

CAMPBELL, Colen, *Vitruvius Britannicus*, London, 1715–25 (3 vols)

COLVIN, H.M., *A Biographical Dictionary of British Architects, 1600–1840*, London, 1978

COLVIN, H.M., (ed.), *The History of the King's Works*, London, 1963–81

G.E.C. and others (eds), *The Complete Peerage*, London, 1910–59 (13 vols)

COOPER, Lady Diana, *Autobiography*, Wilton, 1978

Country Life: various articles

DEVONSHIRE, 6th DUKE OF, *Handbook to Chatsworth and Hardwick*, London, 1844

DEVONSHIRE, DUCHESS OF, *The House*, London, 1982

—— *The Estate*, London, 1990

—— *Treasures of Chatsworth*, London, 1991

—— *Chatsworth*, Derby, 1992

—— *The Garden at Chatsworth*, London, 1999

Dictionary of National Biography

DOWNES, Kerry, *English Baroque Architecture*, London, 1966

—— *Hawksmoor*, London, 1970

—— *Vanbrugh*, London, 1979

EGREMONT, Lord, *Wyndham and Children First*, London, 1968

FEDDEN, Robert, and KENWORTHY-BROWNE, John, *The Country House Guide*, London, 1979

FIELDING, Daphne, *Mercury Presides*, London, 1954

GIROUARD, Mark, *The Victorian Country House*, Oxford, 1971, and New Haven and London, 1979

—— *Life in the English Country House*, New Haven and London, 1978

—— *Historic Houses of Britain*, London, 1979

—— *Robert Smythson and the Elizabethan Country House*, New Haven and London, 1983

GREEN, David, *Blenheim Palace*, London, 1951

—— *Grinling Gibbons*, London, 1964

—— *Sarah Duchess of Marlborough*, London, 1967

—— *The Churchills of Blenheim*, London, 1984

GREEVES, Lydia, and TRINICK, Michael, *The National Trust Guide*, London, 1989 (4th edn)

HARE, Augustus, *The Story of My Life*, London, 1896–1900 (6 vols)

HARRIS, John, *Sir William Chambers*, London, 1970

HERBERT, David, *Second Son*, London, 1972

HILL, Oliver, and CORNFORTH, John, *English Country Houses: Caroline*, London, 1966 (also other titles in this series)

HUSSEY, Christopher, *English Country Houses Open to the Public*, London, 1951

—— *English Country Houses: Early Georgian, 1715–60*, London, 1955

—— *English Country Houses: Mid-Georgian, 1760–1800*, London, 1956

—— *English Country Houses: Late Georgian, 1800–40*, London, 1958

JACKSON-STOPS, Gervase, *The English Country House: A Grand Tour*, London, 1985

—— *The Country House in Perspective*, London, 1990

JACKSON-STOPS, Gervase (ed.), *Treasure Houses of Britain*, New Haven and London, 1985

KETTON-CREMER, R.W., *Horace Walpole*, London, 1964

MARKHAM, Sarah, *John Loveday of Caversham*, Wilton, 1984

MONTGOMERY-MASSINGBERD, Hugh, *Blenheim Revisited*, London, 1985

—— *Great British Families*, London and Exeter, 1988

MONTGOMERY-MASSINGBERD, Hugh (ed.), *Guide to Country Houses*, London, 1978–91 (4 vols)

MASTERS, Brian, *The Dukes*, London, 1975 and 1980

LEES-MILNE, James, *The Age of Adam*, London, 1947

—— *National Trust Guide: Buildings*, London, 1948

—— *Tudor Renaissance*, London, 1951

—— *The Age of Inigo Jones*, London, 1953

—— *English Country Houses: Baroque, 1685–1714*, London, 1970

—— *Ancestral Voices*, London, 1975

—— *The Country House*, Oxford, 1982

—— *Caves of Ice*, London, 1983

—— *Midway on the Waves*, London, 1985

—— *The Bachelor Duke*, London, 1991

—— *People and Places*, London, 1992

NICOLSON, Nigel, *Great Houses of Britain*, London, 1965 and 1978

PEVSNER, Sir Nikolaus *et al*, *The Buildings of England*, London, 1950 (various vols and edns)

POWELL, Anthony (ed.), John Aubrey, *Brief Lives and other Selected Writings*, London, 1949

ROBINSON, John Martin, *The Wyatts*, Oxford, 1979

—— *The Architecture of Northern England*, London, 1986

—— *The English Country Estate*, London, 1988

—— *The Country House at War*, London, 1989

ROSE, Kenneth, *Superior Person*, London, 1969

ROTHSCHILD, Mrs James de, *The Rothschilds at Waddesdon Manor*, London, 1979

ROWSE, A.L., *The Later Churchills*, London, 1958

SACKVILLE-WEST, V., *The Edwardians*, London, 1922

—— *Knole and the Sackvilles*, London, 1922

—— *English Country Houses*, London, 1946

SAYER, Michael, and MONTGOMERY-MASSINGBERD, Hugh, *The Disintegration of A Heritage*, Wilby, 1993

SEDGWICK, Romney (ed.), Lord Hervey, *Memoirs*, London, 1952

SITWELL, Sacheverell, *British Architects and Craftsmen*, London, 1964

STEWART, A.F., (ed.), Horace Walpole, *Last Journals*, London, 1910

STRONG, Roy, BINNEY, Marcus, HARRIS, John *et al*, *The Destruction of the Country House*, London, 1974

STROUD, Dorothy, *Humphry Repton*, London, 1962

—— *Henry Holland*, London, 1966

—— *Capability Brown*, London, 1975

SYKES, Christopher Simon, *Black Sheep*, London, 1982

—— *Ancient English Houses*, 1988

VICKERS, Hugo, *Gladys, Duchess of Marlborough*, London, 1979

—— *Cecil Beaton*, London, 1985

WALPOLE, Horace, *Memoirs of the Reign of King George III*, London, 1894 (4 vols)

WAUGH, Evelyn, *Brideshead Revisited*, London, 1945 and 1959

WHISTLER, Laurence, *Sir John Vanbrugh*, London, 1938

—— *The Imagination of Vanbrugh*, London, 1954

YARWOOD, Doreen, *Robert Adam*, London, 1970

INDEX